Verbal Reasoning

& Comprehension

For the CEM (Durham University) test

The 11+
Study Book

and Parents' Guide

This book contains two pull-out sections:

A **Benchmark Test** at the front
A **Parents' Guide to 11+ Verbal Reasoning** at the back

Read the text, then answer the questions that follow.

It was a hot afternoon, and the railway carriage was correspondingly sultry, and the next stop was at Templecombe, nearly an hour ahead. The occupants of the carriage were a small girl, and a smaller girl, and a small boy. An aunt belonging to the children occupied one corner seat, and the further corner seat on the opposite side was occupied by a bachelor who was a stranger to their
5   party, but the small girls and the small boy emphatically occupied the compartment. Both the aunt and the children were conversational in a limited, persistent way, reminding one of the attentions of a housefly that refuses to be discouraged. Most of the aunt's remarks seemed to begin with "Don't," and nearly all of the children's remarks began with "Why?" The bachelor said nothing out loud.
"Don't, Cyril, don't," exclaimed the aunt, as the small boy began smacking the cushions of the seat,
10   producing a cloud of dust at each blow.
"Come and look out of the window," she added.
The child moved reluctantly to the window. "Why are those sheep being driven out of that field?" he asked.
"I expect they are being driven to another field where there is more grass," said the aunt weakly.
15   "But there is lots of grass in that field," protested the boy; "there's nothing else but grass there. Aunt, there's lots of grass in that field."
"Perhaps the grass in the other field is better," suggested the aunt fatuously.
"Why is it better?" came the swift, inevitable question.
"Oh, look at those cows!" exclaimed the aunt. Nearly every field along the line had contained
20   cows or bullocks, but she spoke as though she were drawing attention to a rarity.
"Why is the grass in the other field better?" persisted Cyril.
The frown on the bachelor's face was deepening to a scowl. He was a hard, unsympathetic man, the aunt decided in her mind. She was utterly unable to come to any satisfactory decision about the grass in the other field.

An extract from 'The Storyteller' by Saki

1. How many people were travelling in the railway carriage?
    A Three   **B** Four   **C** Five   **D** Six

2. Which word best describes the bachelor's reaction to what's happening in the carriage?
    A Amused   **B** Intrigued   **C** Irritated   **D** Bored

3. Why do you think the aunt pointed out the cows to the boy?
    A To distract him   **B** To impress him   **C** To amuse him   **D** To punish him

4. What is Cyril like?
    A Impatient   **B** Inquisitive   **C** Ignorant   **D** Disobedient

5. Which word does not describe the aunt?
    A Judgemental   **B** Talkative   **C** Exasperated   **D** Proud

6. The family's behaviour is compared to that of a housefly. This image shows how they:
    A talked.   **B** ate.   **C** looked.   **D** played.

7. What does the word "inevitable" mean (line 18)?
    A Difficult   **B** Certain   **C** Tedious   **D** Final

Complete the word on the right so it means the opposite of the word on the left.

8. Give   ☐ e c ☐ ☐ v e   9. Perfect   ☐ ☐ a ☐ e d

Underline the word that means the same, or nearly the same, as the word on the left.

10. **GOOD**   circumspect   awry   virtuous   straight

11. **ALLOW**   accept   withhold   confirm   commit

12. **LONG**   stretch   yearn   yield   persevere

/12

END OF TEST

VHRDE1

Read the text, then answer the questions that follow.

Of all the unpopular monarchs in English history, King John's reputation for cruelty sets him apart from the rest, and he has even become known as 'Bad King John'.

John was the youngest of five sons, so he was never expected to become king. He grew up constantly in the shadow of his well-respected, courageous older brother, 'Richard the Lionheart'.
5 John was a greedy man who was hungry for power, so he was very jealous when Richard became king. Richard soon realised that his brother was a threat and made John promise to stay away from England to prevent him from stealing his throne.

However, while Richard was fighting wars abroad, John attempted to seize the English throne in his brother's absence. He spread false rumours throughout England that Richard had died in battle.
10 John's plot eventually failed when his army surrendered to Richard's men and John was forced to ask his brother for forgiveness for his treachery.

When Richard died in 1199, John became king at last, although he had lost his people's trust. He was known as a heartless man, and people said that he had murdered his own nephew, who wanted to take John's throne. Compared to Richard, John's reign was unsuccessful in many ways:
15 he lost land in France, increased taxes and argued with the Pope in Rome.

In 1216, while fighting a war against his own people, John suddenly became ill and died. Although he reigned about 800 years ago, his legacy lives on in English folklore, in the legend of Robin Hood and other stories set at that time.

---

1. John was not expected to become king because he:

   A hated Richard. **B** was the youngest son. **C** was nasty. **D** was weak.

2. For what did John ask Richard's forgiveness?

   A Murder   **B** Telling lies   **C** Trying to steal the crown   **D** Coming to England

3. How did the English people feel when John came to the throne?

   A Afraid   **B** Angry   **C** Threatened   **D** Suspicious

4. Which word best describes how John felt about Richard?

   A Indifferent   **B** Envious   **C** Afraid   **D** Respectful

5. Which of these is given as a reason for thinking that King John was a bad monarch?

   A He was a liar. **B** He was cruel. **C** He was violent. **D** He stole land.

6. According to the passage, which word describes Richard?

   A Brave   **B** Sensible   **C** Arrogant   **D** Intelligent

7. What does the word "constantly" mean (line 4)?

   A Certainly   **B** Mostly   **C** Always   **D** Regularly

Underline the word that means the opposite, or nearly the opposite, of the word on the left.

8. **CURLY**   wavy   straight   uneven   hard

9. **LOOSEN**   slacken   wobbly   adjust   squeeze

10. **FEW**   many   solo   seldom   enough

Underline the correct word to complete each sentence below.

                            swirling
11. Stars and planets are formed from silent   clouds of dust and gas called nebulas.
                            blowing

                  lengthy
12. Skydiving is usually a tedious   experience.
                  thrilling

/12

11+ Verbal Reasoning — Benchmark Test

There are 36 questions in this test and it should take about 20 minutes. Circle the correct answer to each question. If you get stuck on a question, move on to the next one.

Read the text, then answer the questions that follow.

Adam had been looking forward to his eighth birthday for months. It was a hot, sunny day and the sky was blue. Best of all, there was no school because all the teachers were away on a course.

Adam's mum worked during the day, writing articles for a local newspaper. Adam's dad cleaned the house, washed the clothes and did the shopping. So it was his dad who took Adam into town to

5   buy his birthday present — a new pair of trainers.

Adam looked around eagerly when they got to the shop. The trainers he chose were brilliant white with red lightning flashes and they fitted perfectly. He proudly showed them to Mum as soon as she got home.

"They look great, Adam, but I bet they won't stay that white for long," Mum chuckled.

10   That evening, Dad cooked a special birthday dinner, then afterwards Adam went out to play with his friend, Mahir. He had pleaded with Mum and Dad to let him wear his new trainers. They had agreed, as long as he was careful to keep them clean, but he was too busy having fun with Mahir to worry about that. They chased each other through the woods, played football, pushed each other on the swings and then raced home again.

15   As Adam walked through the door, he looked at his trainers. They were filthy and scuffed, and suddenly he felt bad about getting them so dirty. What would his parents say?

1. What colour were Adam's new trainers?

   A White   **B** Red   **C** Red and white   **D** Blue

2. What job does Adam's mum do?

   A Journalist   **B** Cleaner   **C** Secretary   **D** Teacher

3. Which of these activities does Adam not do with Mahir?

   A Play football   **B** Play chase   **C** Climb trees   **D** Play on the swings

4. According to the text, there was no school because it was:

   A Saturday.   **B** the holidays.   **C** summer.   **D** a training day.

5. Which of these is not mentioned in the text?

   A Cooking   **B** Cleaning   **C** Washing clothes   **D** Ironing clothes

6. How does Adam feel at the end of his birthday?

   A Excited   **B** Guilty   **C** Proud   **D** Tired

7. What does the word "pleaded" mean (line 11)?

   A Told   **B** Begged   **C** Argued   **D** Cried

Three of the words in each list are linked. Underline the word that is **not** related to the other three.

8. mountain   cliff   hill   field

9. stone   water   pebble   rock

10. zebra   giraffe   hippo   dog

Complete the word on the right so it means the same as the word on the left.

11. Big   [ ][u][g][ ]   12. Castle   [f][ ][r][ ]

/12

CGP

Verbal Reasoning
& Comprehension

The 11+
Study Book

and Parents' Guide

For the CEM (Durham University) test

Practise • Prepare • Pass

Everything your child needs for 11+ success

CONTENTS

Section Three — Completing Passages

Section Four — Comprehension

Published by CGP

Editors:
Claire Boulter, Julie Wakeling

Reviewer:
Alison Griffin

With thanks to Rebecca Tate and Luke von Kotze for the proofreading.

With thanks to the moderators of ElevenPlusExams.co.uk for their input.

Please note that CGP is not associated with CEM or The University of Durham in any way.
This book does not include any official questions and it is not endorsed by CEM or The University of Durham.
CEM, Centre for Evaluation and Monitoring, Durham University and
The University of Durham are all trademarks of The University of Durham.

ISBN: 978 1 84762 161 0
Printed by Elanders Ltd, Newcastle upon Tyne.
Clipart from Corel®

Based on the classic CGP style created by Richard Parsons.

What's in the 11+

Here's a quick overview of what's in the 11+ to help you get your head round the basics.

The **11+** is an **Admissions Test**

1) The 11+ is a test used by <u>some schools</u> to help with their <u>selection process</u>.
2) You'll usually take it when you're in <u>Year 6</u>, at some point during the <u>autumn term</u>.
3) Schools <u>use the results</u> to decide who to accept. They might also use <u>other things</u> to help make up their mind, like information about <u>where you live</u>.

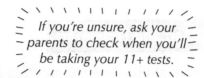

If you're unsure, ask your parents to check when you'll be taking your 11+ tests.

You'll be tested on a **Mixture** of **Subjects**

1) In your 11+, you'll be tested on <u>these subjects</u>:

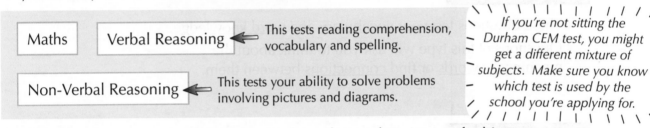

Maths

Verbal Reasoning ← This tests reading comprehension, vocabulary and spelling.

Non-Verbal Reasoning ← This tests your ability to solve problems involving pictures and diagrams.

If you're not sitting the Durham CEM test, you might get a different mixture of subjects. Make sure you know which test is used by the school you're applying for.

2) You'll probably sit <u>two 45 minute tests</u>, each made up of a mixture of subjects.
3) This book will help you with the <u>Verbal Reasoning</u> part of the test.

Get to **Know** what **Kinds** of **Questions** you might get

Most of the questions in your test will be <u>multiple choice</u> but for some you might have to write your answer yourself.

Look out for the 'Tips and Tricks' boxes in this Study Book — they'll give you practical advice about the test.

Multiple Choice

1) For each question you'll be given some <u>options</u> on the <u>question paper</u>.
2) You should draw a clear pencil <u>line</u> in the box next to the <u>option</u> that you think is <u>correct</u>.
3) You might have to mark your answers on a <u>separate answer sheet</u>.

Fill in the Blanks

You'll have to <u>fill in</u> some <u>boxes</u> to answer these questions. Here's an example:

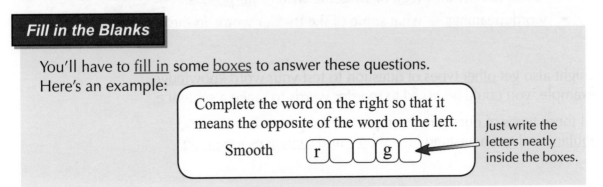

Complete the word on the right so that it means the opposite of the word on the left.

Smooth   r ☐ ☐ g ☐

Just write the letters neatly inside the boxes.

What's in the 11+ Verbal Reasoning Test

Get your brain ready for Verbal Reasoning by reading about the different question types.

Verbal Reasoning tests your *Reading* and *Word Knowledge*

1) You'll already have <u>picked up</u> loads of the <u>skills</u> you need <u>at school</u>.

2) There are four <u>main types</u> of <u>questions</u> that can crop up:

Spelling and Grammar

You might be asked to <u>proofread</u> a passage — you'll have to <u>spot</u> and <u>correct</u> spelling and grammar mistakes.

Word Meanings

These questions test your <u>vocabulary</u> and <u>word knowledge</u>. Questions of this type will ask you to think about the <u>meanings of words</u> or find <u>connections</u> between them.

Cloze Passages

It's likely that you'll be given one <u>long</u> or several <u>short</u> cloze passages in your test. Each cloze passage is a text with some <u>bits missing</u>. You'll either have to choose some words to fill the <u>gaps</u>, or fill in the <u>missing letters</u> in some of the words. To do this you'll need to be able to <u>spell</u> words correctly, and have a good grasp of <u>grammar</u>.

Comprehension

You'll probably be given one <u>long</u> text or several <u>short</u> texts to read. You'll have to answer <u>questions</u> which test how well you <u>understand</u> the text. The questions might ask you about:

- what the text <u>means</u> — what <u>happens</u> in the text, what a <u>character</u> is like or how they <u>feel</u>, or what the writer's <u>purpose</u> is.
- <u>word meanings</u> — what some of the trickier words in the text <u>mean</u>.

3) You might also get <u>other types</u> of question to test your <u>word knowledge</u>. For example, you could be asked to <u>reorder words</u> to make a sentence.

4) For all these types of question, it's important for you to have a <u>good</u> <u>vocabulary</u> and to understand how <u>words</u> and <u>sentences</u> are <u>made</u>.

How to Prepare for the 11+

Give yourself a head start with your Verbal Reasoning preparation — be organised and plan ahead.

Divide your Preparation into Stages

1) You should find a way to prepare for the 11+ that <u>suits you</u>. This may depend on <u>how much time</u> you have before the test. Here's a good way to <u>plan</u> your Verbal Reasoning practice:

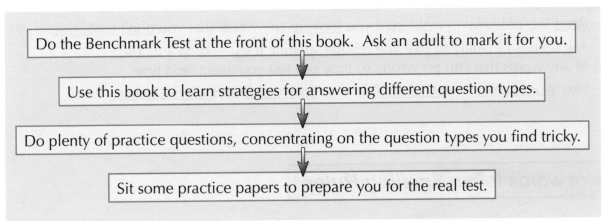

Do the Benchmark Test at the front of this book. Ask an adult to mark it for you.

Use this book to learn strategies for answering different question types.

Do plenty of practice questions, concentrating on the question types you find tricky.

Sit some practice papers to prepare you for the real test.

2) When you <u>first</u> start answering Verbal Reasoning questions, try to solve the questions without <u>making any mistakes</u>, rather than working <u>quickly</u>.

3) Once you feel <u>confident</u> about the questions, then you can build up your <u>speed</u>.

4) You can do this by asking an adult to <u>time</u> you as you answer a <u>set of questions</u>, or by seeing <u>how many</u> questions you can answer in a certain <u>amount of time</u>, e.g. 5 minutes. You can then try to <u>beat</u> your time or score.

5) As you get closer to the test day, work on getting a <u>balance</u> between <u>speed</u> and <u>accuracy</u> — that's what you're <u>aiming for</u> when you sit the real test.

There are Many Ways to Practise the Skills you Need

The <u>best way</u> to tackle Verbal Reasoning is to do lots of <u>practice</u>. This isn't the only thing that will help though — there are other ways you can <u>build up the skills</u> you need for the test:

1) Read a mix of <u>fiction</u> and <u>non-fiction</u> — <u>poetry</u>, <u>newspapers</u>, <u>novels</u> etc.

2) If you come across any <u>unfamiliar words</u>, look them up in a <u>dictionary</u>. Keeping a <u>vocabulary list</u> is a great way to <u>remember</u> new words.

3) If you're reading an <u>article</u> in a newspaper or magazine, <u>underline</u> the <u>key facts</u> as you read — picking out the most <u>important information</u> from a text is a really <u>useful skill</u>.

4) Play <u>word games</u> or do <u>crosswords</u> to build up your <u>vocabulary</u>.

5) Play games like 'Twenty Questions' or 'Cluedo' to help you <u>think logically</u> and <u>draw conclusions</u> based on information that you're given.

Preparing for the Test

Make sure you know how words are made — it'll help you in your test.

Verbal Reasoning Questions test your Spelling

Many verbal reasoning questions test your <u>word recognition</u> and your <u>spelling skills</u>. You can <u>improve</u> these skills in a couple of ways:

1) <u>Read</u> lots of books — make sure you <u>look up</u> any words that you <u>don't recognise</u>.
2) Ask friends or family to give you <u>regular spelling tests</u> — keep a <u>record</u> of any words that you get <u>wrong</u> so they can test you again <u>next time</u>.
3) Play <u>word games</u> like SCRABBLE® or do <u>crosswords</u> and <u>wordsearches</u>.

Lots of words follow Spelling Rules

Whether you're <u>looking for spelling errors</u> or <u>completing words</u> in a cloze question (see Section Three), it'll help if you can <u>recognise common spelling patterns</u>.

Patterns at the *Start* of words

1) Words can <u>start</u> with <u>any letter</u> of the alphabet, but not <u>any combination of letters</u>.
2) You'll see 'b', 'c', 'f', 'g', 'p' or 't' <u>before</u> 'l' or 'r', but <u>never after</u> 'l' or 'r' at the <u>start of a word</u>.

<u>bl</u>ow, <u>cr</u>own, <u>fl</u>ip, <u>gr</u>ab, <u>pl</u>ot, <u>tr</u>ip   lb✗   rb✗   lc✗   rc✗   lf✗   rf✗   lg✗   rg✗   lp✗   rp✗   rt✗

3) '<u>h</u>' is common after '<u>c</u>', '<u>s</u>', '<u>t</u>' and '<u>w</u>'. ⇒ <u>ch</u>ip, <u>sh</u>op, <u>th</u>is, <u>wh</u>en

4) A <u>prefix</u> (see p.10) can be added to the <u>start</u> of a word to <u>change</u> its <u>meaning</u>, for example:

un- (unlock, untidy)   dis- (disappear, dislike)   in- (inedible, indescribable)

Patterns in the *Middle* of words

1) Almost all words contain <u>vowels</u>. Some patterns of vowels appear <u>frequently</u>, for example:

ee oo ou ie ea   s<u>ee</u>n l<u>oo</u>k p<u>ou</u>t d<u>ie</u>t t<u>ea</u>r

2) Some vowels <u>rarely</u> appear together, for example, '<u>uo</u>', '<u>iu</u>', '<u>ae</u>'.

3) <u>Double consonants</u> (see p.12) in the <u>middle of words</u> are common — you'll often come across '<u>tt</u>', '<u>ss</u>' or '<u>pp</u>', but it's less likely ⇒ you'll see a word with '<u>hh</u>', '<u>vv</u>', '<u>jj</u>', '<u>ww</u>' or '<u>xx</u>'.

bu<u>tt</u>er a<u>ss</u>ume sto<u>pp</u>ing

4) If you can recognise common <u>vowel</u> and <u>consonant</u> patterns that appear in the middle of words, such as '<u>per</u>', '<u>our</u>', '<u>are</u>' and '<u>ate</u>', it'll help to improve your <u>spelling</u>.

Patterns at the **End** of words

1) Some <u>combinations</u> of <u>consonants</u> are often found at the <u>end</u> of words. For <u>example</u>:

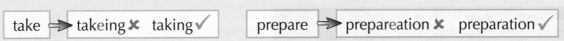

| church | clock | fifth | cash | harm | high | string |

2) <u>Suffixes</u> (see p.10) come at the <u>end</u> of words — they can be <u>verb</u> endings like '<u>-ed</u>', <u>plurals</u> such as '<u>-s</u>' or <u>adverb</u> endings like '<u>-ly</u>'. Here are some <u>common suffixes</u>:

| -ition (addition) | -ity (humidity) | -ful (careful) | -ing (playing) | -y (sandy) |

3) Remember, when you <u>add a suffix</u> the <u>spelling</u> of the root word can <u>change</u>:

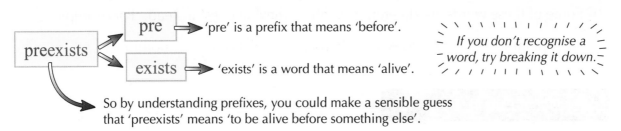

take ➡ takeing ✗ taking ✓   prepare ➡ prepareation ✗ preparation ✓

Use **Spelling Patterns** to help you answer questions

1) If you know a bit about <u>prefixes</u> it can help you work out the <u>meaning</u> of words, for example:

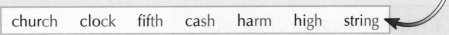

preexists

pre ➡ 'pre' is a prefix that means 'before'.

exists ➡ 'exists' is a word that means 'alive'.

If you don't recognise a word, try breaking it down.

So by understanding prefixes, you could make a sensible guess that 'preexists' means 'to be alive before something else'.

2) Learn some common <u>patterns</u> in the <u>middle</u> of words — it'll help with your <u>spelling</u>.

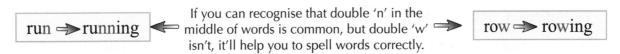

run ➡ running ⬅ If you can recognise that double 'n' in the middle of words is common, but double 'w' isn't, it'll help you to spell words correctly. ➡ row ➡ rowing

---

Practice Questions

1) Find three prefixes other than un-, dis- and in-.

2) Can you think of any words that start with the following letters?
   a) str   b) blr   c) shr   d) ds

3) Write the correct spelling of each of these words.
   a) anywere   b) stuborn   c) hovvercraft   d) shipwrec

4) Write out each of these root words with the prefix or suffix added.
   a) un + natural   b) angry + ly   c) mis + spell   d) vaccine + ate

Plurals

Plural means 'more than one'. So here's a plural number of pages about plurals. Enjoy...

Add 's' to make Most Words plural

<u>Most plurals</u> are formed by adding an '<u>s</u>':

mask ⟹ masks

Monday ⟹ Mondays

Other words have Different Rules

Words that End in 'ch', 'sh', 's', 'x' and 'z'

1) Put '<u>es</u>' at the <u>end</u> of words ending in <u>these letters</u>.
2) You need to add the 'es' to make sure that you keep the soft sound in the <u>original word</u>.

kiss ⟹ kisses

watch ⟹ watches

Words that End in 'o'

1) Words that end in '<u>o</u>' <u>usually</u> need '<u>s</u>' to make their plural, e.g. pianos, discos.
2) Some of these words are <u>different</u> though — they take '<u>es</u>' instead. For example:

| potatoes | tomatoes | heroes | echoes | dominoes |

Words that End in 'f' and 'fe'

1) You need to add '<u>ves</u>' to many words that end in '<u>f</u>' and '<u>fe</u>' to make them plural.

loaf ⟹ loaves   shelf ⟹ shelves   wife ⟹ wives

2) But again, some are <u>different</u>. These words just need an '<u>s</u>':

| chiefs | chefs | beliefs | reefs | giraffes | cliffs |

Words that End in 'y'

1) If the letter <u>before</u> the 'y' is a <u>vowel</u>, just add '<u>s</u>' to make the plural:

toy ⟹ toys

2) If the letter <u>before</u> the 'y' is a <u>consonant</u>, the 'y' becomes '<u>ies</u>' for the plural:

daisy ⟹ daisies

Vowels are the letters 'a', 'e', 'i', 'o' and 'u'. All the other letters of the alphabet are consonants.

Irregular Plurals

These words all change their <u>vowel sound</u> when they become plural:

| tooth ⟹ teeth | woman ⟹ women | mouse ⟹ mice |
| man ⟹ men | goose ⟹ geese | oasis ⟹ oases |

You may be asked to **Choose** the **Correct Plural**

Q Circle the correct plural to complete each sentence below.

a) My family owns three *stereoes / stereoss / stereos / steroes*.
b) The clown at the circus was juggling with *knifes / kniffs / knifies / knives*.
c) My sister still believes in *faires / fairies / fairys / faireys*.
d) We have *mouses / mice / mise / mousies* living under the floorboards.

Method — Follow the rules for making plurals

1) Follow the <u>rules</u> to work out the <u>plurals</u>.
2) Remember to look out for any <u>exceptions</u> to the rules (see the previous page).

a) My family owns three *stereoes / stereoss /* (*stereos*) */ steroes*.

The word 'stereo' ends in 'o', so the plural ending has to be 's' or 'es'. → 'Stereo' takes the 's' ending — so the correct plural is 'stereos'.

b) The clown at the circus was juggling with *knifes / kniffs / knifies /* (*knives*)

'Knife' has an 'fe' ending. Many words ending in 'fe' take the plural 'ves', but some end in 's'. → The plural of 'knife' takes the more common 'ves' ending, so the answer is 'knives'.

c) My sister still believes in *faires /* (*fairies*) */ fairys / faireys*.

'Fairy' ends with a 'y', so you need to look at the letter before the 'y' to work out the correct plural ending. → The letter before the 'y' is a consonant — 'r'. So the plural of 'fairy' is 'fairies'.

d) We have *mouses /* (*mice*) */ mise / mousies* living under the floorboards.

The vowel sound of 'mouse' changes when it becomes plural. → The correct plural form of 'mouse' is 'mice'.

Tips and Tricks for Writing Plurals

You might have to complete plurals in the test — make sure you follow the rules for forming plurals, but remember the exceptions.

Practice Questions

1) Fill in the gap in each sentence, using the correct plural form of the word in brackets.

a) We watched the monkey swing from the .... (*branch*) of the tree.
b) My .... (*foot*) were wet after I ran through the puddle.
c) We're spending Christmas with the .... (*Grady*). ← *This one is asking for the plural of a name.*
d) I heard two .... (*wolf*) howling in the forest.
e) Would you like to try on any of those .... (*dress*)?

Homophones and Homographs

Don't be put off by these complicated words — you probably know loads of homophones already.

Warm-Up Activity

For each of the words below, write down another word
that sounds exactly the same, but is spelt differently.

piece   waist   or   sale   sight   male

Homophones sound the Same

1) Homophones are words that sound the same, but mean different things.
2) Here are lots of examples:

bean and been	root and route	weather and whether
pair and pear	rap and wrap	there, their and they're
wait and weight	blue and blew	by, buy and bye
maid and made	hire and higher	allowed and aloud
peer and pier	boy and buoy	principle and principal

Homographs have the Same Spelling

Homographs don't always sound the same.

1) Homographs are words that have the same spelling but a different meaning.
2) Here is an example:

| You need a bow and arrow to be an archer. | Remember to bow to the queen. |

The word 'bow' has two different meanings in these sentences.
You only know which meaning it is by reading the rest of the sentence.

A Pun is a Play on Words

Jokes that use homophones are called puns.

What do rabbits use to comb their fur? A hare brush.

Here 'hare' (an animal like a rabbit) is used
instead of 'hair'. The two words are homophones.

I'm on a seafood diet — I see food and I eat it.

Seafood includes things
like fish and prawns.

'See food' and 'seafood'
are homophones.

Make sure you know the *Meanings* of common **Homophones**

 Q Circle the correct homophone to complete each sentence below.

a) The supermarket is down by the *quay / key*.
b) My dog has lovely long *fir / fur*.
c) My arm was feeling very *saw / sore* when I woke up this morning.
d) I can't *bear / bare* another day at school today.

Method — Look closely at the spelling of the homophones

1) Work out the <u>meaning</u> of the homophones in each sentence.
2) Then choose the <u>correct</u> homophone to <u>fit</u> the meaning of the sentence.

a) The supermarket is down by the (quay) / key.

A 'quay' is an area along a waterfront.
It's somewhere that you may find a supermarket.

You open a lock using a 'key'.
This meaning doesn't fit the sentence.

b) My dog has lovely long *fir* / (fur)

'fir' is a type of tree.

'fur' is the hair on animals. This is the
correct homophone for the sentence.

c) My arm was feeling very *saw* / (sore) when I woke up this morning.

'saw' could be the past tense of 'see'
or a tool used for cutting wood.

'sore' means 'sensitive' and 'painful'. This is
the correct answer — it fits in the sentence.

d) I can't (bear) / bare another day at school today.

'bear' is an animal, but it also means 'to
endure' — this meaning fits the sentence.

'bare' means 'naked'
or 'sparse'.

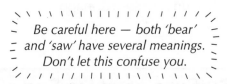
*Be careful here — both 'bear'
and 'saw' have several meanings.
Don't let this confuse you.*

Practice Questions

1) Circle the homophones that have been used incorrectly in the passage below.

*I'm supposed to go to drama group every Monday knight, but this weak I'm too tired.
I've had a very busy day at school and I'm not feeling grate. Instead, I think I'm
going to stay hear and watch a film that I haven't scene before.*

2) Circle the correct homophone to complete each sentence below.
a) Make sure that you know *wear / where* you are going.
b) Watch out for the crab — it has very sharp *claws / clause*.
c) At the theme park, we *road / rode* on four different roller coasters.
d) The jockey pulled on the *reigns / reins* to get the horse to stop.

Prefixes and Suffixes

Don't get your fixes in a twist — learn how to use prefixes and suffixes for the test...

Warm-Up Activity

Match the prefixes and suffixes to the correct words.
One has been done for you — 're' and 'match' make 'rematch'.

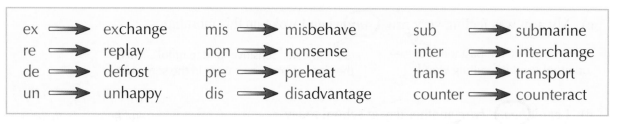

match   un   available   re   work

er   thought   ly   formal   ful

Prefixes go at the Start of Words

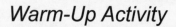

Remember — 'pre' = 'before', so prefixes always go at the start of words.

1) Add a prefix at the <u>start</u> of a word to make a <u>new word</u>.

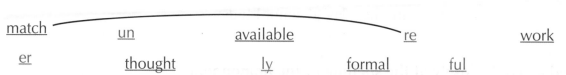

ground ⟹ underground

The word that you add the prefix to is called the <u>root word</u>.

'under' is the prefix

clockwise ⟹ anticlockwise

'anti' is the prefix

2) Here are some <u>common prefixes</u> and an example of a word that uses each one:

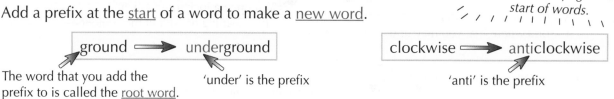

ex ⟹ exchange	mis ⟹ misbehave	sub ⟹ submarine
re ⟹ replay	non ⟹ nonsense	inter ⟹ interchange
de ⟹ defrost	pre ⟹ preheat	trans ⟹ transport
un ⟹ unhappy	dis ⟹ disadvantage	counter ⟹ counteract

Suffixes go at the End of Words

1) Add a suffix to the <u>end</u> of a word to make a <u>new word</u>.

garden ⟹ gardener

'garden' is the root word.

'er' is the suffix

turn ⟹ turning

'ing' is the suffix

2) Here's a list of <u>common suffixes</u> with a <u>word</u> that uses each one:

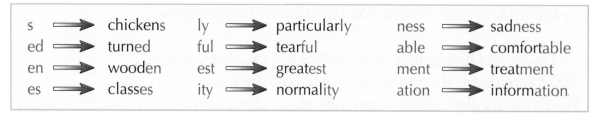

s ⟹ chickens	ly ⟹ particularly	ness ⟹ sadness
ed ⟹ turned	ful ⟹ tearful	able ⟹ comfortable
en ⟹ wooden	est ⟹ greatest	ment ⟹ treatment
es ⟹ classes	ity ⟹ normality	ation ⟹ information

3) Sometimes adding a suffix can <u>change the spelling</u> of the word:

travel ⟹ traveller   stop ⟹ stopping   take ⟹ taking

You could be asked to write the **Correct Prefix** or **Suffix**

Q Write the correct prefix or suffix to complete the words in the sentences.

a) I asked the waiter for a ☐☐fill of my soft drink.

b) It was ☐☐fortunate that you missed the last train home.

c) The travell☐☐☐ left the airport an hour late after their flight was delayed.

d) Angus is the tall☐☐☐ boy in school.

Method — Read through each sentence carefully

1) You need to add a <u>prefix</u> to parts a) and b). Make sure that the prefix <u>agrees</u> with the meaning of the <u>rest</u> of the sentence.

a) I asked the waiter for a [r][e]fill of my soft drink.

The speaker is asking for another drink.
The word is 'refill', so the correct prefix is 're'.

b) It was [u][n]fortunate that you missed the last train home.

The sentence is talking about having bad luck,
so the correct prefix to add is 'un' to make 'unfortunate'.

2) Look at the <u>whole sentence</u> in parts c) and d) to help you choose the correct <u>suffix</u>.

c) The travell[e][r][s] left the airport an hour late after their flight was delayed.

You need to add a plural suffix here as the sentence talks
about a group of people. Add 'ers' to make 'travellers'.

'their' tells you that it was
more than one person.

d) Angus is the tall[e][s][t] boy in school.

The sentence is about the 'most tall' boy
in school, so the correct suffix is 'est'.

Practice Questions

1) Complete the sentences by adding the correct prefix or suffix to the word in brackets.

a) The baby polar bear is so _____ (*adore*).

b) I was trying to be _____ (*help*) when I washed the dishes.

c) The ball hit Kayley and knocked her _____ (*conscious*).

d) Lyla's feeling of _____ (*happy*) increased when she found her shoes.

e) The apple was covered in mould and the flesh was _____ (*rot*).

The spelling of the root word may change.

Silent Letters and Double Letters

Silent and double letters — making spelling double the fun since 1476...

Warm-Up Activity

A consonant is any letter of the alphabet other than 'a', 'e', 'i', 'o' or 'u'.

Circle the silent <u>consonants</u> in each word.

k n i f e   s c e n e   g n o m e

i s l a n d   w h i l e   l a m b   r h y m e

Some words have **Silent Letters**

1) Some words are not spelt the way they <u>sound</u>. They have <u>silent letters</u> which you don't hear.
2) Here are some <u>common examples</u>:

Words with a *Silent 'h'*

which	whistle	when
choir	chemist	rhino

Words with a *Silent 'k'*

knock	knife	knuckle
knight	know	knowledge

Lots more words have silent letters — these are some of the common ones.

Words with a *Silent 'b'*

comb	numb	debt
tomb	thumb	doubt

Words with a *Silent 'c'*

yacht	science	scissors
scent	rescind	descend

Words with a *Silent 'w'*

write	wrist	wrong
wrap	answer	who

Words with a *Silent 't'*

listen	whistle
thistle	castle

Words with a *Silent 'l'*

salmon	could
would	should

Words with **Double Letters** can be **Tricky**

Try to think of ways to remember these spellings, e.g. 'necessary' could be 'Never Eat Chips; Eat Salad Sandwiches And Remain Young'.

These words have <u>double letters</u> that you say as a <u>single sound</u>:

accommodation	different	exaggerate	occasion
address	disappear	immediately	occurrence
appalling	embarrass	irresistible	possess
association	essential	jewellery	succulent
deterrent	eventually	necessary	succumb

You may have to find **Words** that are **Spelt Wrong**

Q Circle the spelling mistakes in the passage below.

1 *Tomorow morning I leave for an autum trip with my youth group. We woud*
2 *like to go to the Lake District as we usually do, but instead we're going to the*
3 *New Forest. We've got lots of fun acttivities planned like hiking and climing,*
4 *and every knight we will sit by the campfire and eat toasted marshmallows.*

Method — Look for silent letters and double letters

1) Work through the passage <u>one line</u> at a time.

2) Look carefully for words that are <u>missing</u> a silent letter,
   or where double letters are used <u>incorrectly</u> or <u>missing</u>.

(Tomorrow) morning I leave for an (autumn) trip with my youth group. We (would)

'Tomorrow' has a double 'r'.   'autumn' has a silent 'n' at the end.   'would' has a silent 'l'.

like to go to the Lake District as we usually do, but instead we're going to the

There are no spelling mistakes in this line.

New Forest. We've got lots of fun (activities) planned like hiking and (climbing)

A double 't' is not needed after 'c'.   'climbing' has a silent 'b'.
It should be spelt as 'activities'.

and every (night) we will sit by the campfire and eat toasted marshmallows.

This should be 'night' in this context — it isn't spelt
with a silent 'k' when it means the opposite of day.

The context of the sentence should give you clues about how to spell some words.

Practice Questions

1) Each sentence below contains one spelling mistake.
   Rewrite the sentences, using the correct word.
   a) *I maintainned a comfortable position for the whole journey.*
   b) *You need to wear more cloths in winter to keep warm.*
   c) *My interresting entry will win the competition tomorrow.*

2) Rewrite the sentences, using the correct word.
   a) Everyone agreed that the charity event had been *successful / successfull / sucessful*.
   b) While we're in London, we want to visit Nelson's *Colum / Collumn / Column*.
   c) Sasha is the most *intelligent / inteligent / inteliggent* girl in the class.
   d) I arrived just as the show was *begining / beginning / beggining*.

Other Awkward Spellings

Bad news, I'm afraid — there are even more words that don't follow the rules.

The 'i' before 'e' rule

1) Learn this rule — it's <u>important</u>:

> 'i' before 'e' except after 'c', but only when it rhymes with bee.

The whole word doesn't need to rhyme with bee, just the 'ie' sound.

2) Here are some examples:

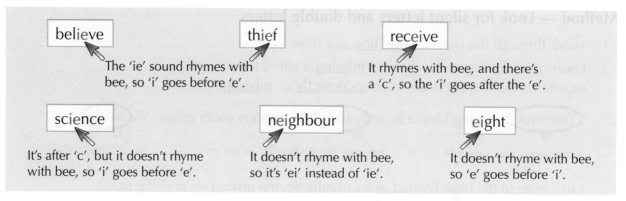

believe — The 'ie' sound rhymes with bee, so 'i' goes before 'e'.

thief — It rhymes with bee, and there's a 'c', so the 'i' goes after the 'e'.

receive — It rhymes with bee, and there's a 'c', so the 'i' goes after the 'e'.

science — It's after 'c', but it doesn't rhyme with bee, so 'i' goes before 'e'.

neighbour — It doesn't rhyme with bee, so it's 'ei' instead of 'ie'.

eight — It doesn't rhyme with bee, so 'e' goes before 'i'.

3) There are a <u>few exceptions</u> to the rule, like '<u>weird</u>' and '<u>seize</u>'.

Unstressed Vowels can make words tricky to spell

1) Sometimes the <u>vowel sound</u> in a word isn't <u>clear</u> — these sounds are called <u>unstressed vowels</u>.

2) Spelling these words can be <u>awkward</u> because the vowels don't make the sound you would <u>expect</u>.

*Make up some short phrases to help you remember how to spell words with unstressed vowels, e.g. "I'm **at** a priv**at**e party".*

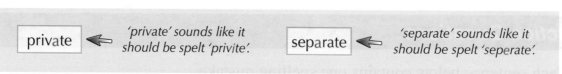

private ← 'private' sounds like it should be spelt 'privite'.

separate ← 'separate' sounds like it should be spelt 'seperate'.

3) Unfortunately there isn't a rule for spelling words with <u>unstressed vowels</u> — you'll just have to <u>learn</u> how to spell them. Here are some examples:

definitely	doctor	occurrence
ridiculous	difference	company
government	animal	interference
general	biscuit	carpet
describe	jewellery	miserable

You may have to **Add Letters** to a **Word**

Q Fill in the missing letters to complete the words in the sentences below.

a) Adam was rel[ ][ ]ved to find his maths homework.

b) There are p[ ][ ]ces of broken glass everywhere.

c) The villain was very dec[ ][ ]tful.

d) I often w[ ][ ]gh my cat to make sure that she is healthy.

Method — Remember the 'i before e' rule

1) Work out the <u>word</u> that is being <u>added</u> to each sentence.

2) Think carefully about the spelling — look at the letters <u>before</u> and <u>after</u> the gap.

a) Adam was rel[i][e]ved to find his maths homework.

The letter before the gap is 'l' and the 'ie' sound in 'relieved' rhymes with bee.

So 'ie' is the correct spelling to use.

b) There are p[i][e]ces of broken glass everywhere.

The letter before the gap is 'p' and the 'ie' sound rhymes with bee.

So 'pieces' should be spelt with an 'ie'.

Don't get confused by the 'c' after the gap — it doesn't matter which letter comes after the 'ie' sound.

c) The villain was very dec[e][i]tful.

The letter before the gap is 'c' and the 'ie' sound rhymes with bee.

This time you need to add 'ei' to spell 'deceitful'.

d) I often w[e][i]gh my cat to make sure that she is healthy.

The letter before the gap is 'w', but the 'ie' sound does not rhyme with bee.

You should add 'ei' to spell 'weigh'.

Practice Questions

1) Circle the correctly spelt word to complete the sentences below.

a) My car is running out of *diesel / deisel*.

b) Don't forget to paint the *cieling / ceiling*.

c) Mr Harris went to the museum to see the *ancient / anceint* remains.

2) The words below are missing unstressed vowels. Write the correct vowel in each gap.

a) desp[ ]rate

b) fact[ ]ry

c) respons[ ]ble

d) harm[ ]ny

e) lit[ ]r[ ]ture

f) pass[ ]ge

Preparing for Word Meaning Questions

Reading the dictionary isn't the only way to pass the VR part of your test — read on for the lowdown...

Word Meanings Questions test your Vocabulary

Vocabulary means 'the set of words you know'. You can increase your vocabulary in a few ways:

1) Read lots of books and articles to help you learn new words.
2) Every time you come across a word you don't know, look it up in a dictionary and jot down the word and its definition in a notebook. Keep adding to the list and look over the words often.
3) Play word games such as SCRABBLE® or do crosswords to get you thinking about word meanings and how words are formed.
4) Do plenty of VR practice questions.

It's important to read lots of different types of books: fiction, non-fiction and poetry as well as newspaper articles.

Practise spotting different Word Types

1) 'Word type' means what category a word belongs to — e.g. noun, verb, adjective or adverb.
2) Here are a few tips to help you work out the word types:

Nouns are people, places or things

1) Concrete nouns are objects and things.

| cow | apple | dog | milk |

2) Abstract nouns are harder to spot — they're things you can't see, hear, taste, touch or smell.

| childhood | freedom | bravery | adventure |

2) Proper nouns are the names of particular people, places or things. They always start with a capital letter.

Heather is going to Rome in July.

Some words belong to more than one word type. E.g. 'I catch fish', 'There's a catch'. 'Catch' is a verb in the first sentence and a noun in the other.

Verbs describe actions

1) A verb can be a doing word like 'dance', or a being word like 'is'.
2) Verbs can go after 'I', 'you', 'he', 'it', 'she' or 'they'.

I play, you dance, they are, it was

Adverbs describe verbs

Adverbs often end in -ly.

quickly, happily, playfully

Adjectives describe nouns

Adjectives sometimes end with -y, -ly, -ing, -ous, -ful or -able.

sandy, friendly, interesting, gorgeous, peaceful, comfortable

Use **Word Type** to work out the **Answer**

<u>Recognising</u> word types can be a useful way of <u>solving</u> some questions in the <u>VR</u> part of your <u>11+ test</u>.

Put a word in a sentence to work out its **Word Type**

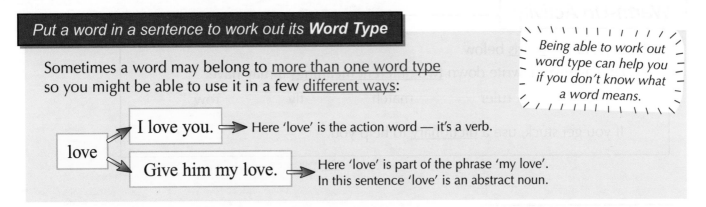

Sometimes a word may belong to <u>more than one word type</u> so you might be able to use it in a few <u>different ways</u>:

Being able to work out word type can help you if you don't know what a word means.

love →

| I love you. | → Here 'love' is the action word — it's a verb. |

| Give him my love. | → Here 'love' is part of the phrase 'my love'. In this sentence 'love' is an abstract noun. |

Look at word endings to help you work out **Word Type**

1) Sometimes you might need to find words that <u>mean the same thing</u>.

2) If you <u>don't recognise</u> some of the words, you could try looking at <u>word type</u> to help you.

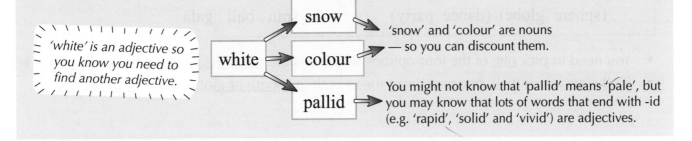

'white' is an adjective so you know you need to find another adjective.

snow

white → colour

'snow' and 'colour' are nouns — so you can discount them.

pallid → You might not know that 'pallid' means 'pale', but you may know that lots of words that end with -id (e.g. 'rapid', 'solid' and 'vivid') are adjectives.

<u>Tips and Tricks</u>

You'll recognise a lot of the words in your VR test — but they like to sneak in some tricky words to test you. If you get one you don't know — don't worry. Try to eliminate any of the other possible answers and, if all else fails, make a sensible guess.

Practice Questions

1) Work out the word type of each of the following words:

a) sang b) honesty c) nosy d) tighten e) cryptic f) play g) vacantly

2) Write down the meaning and word type of the following words.

a) truth b) cantankerous c) wrathfully d) bemusement

Check your answers in a dictionary.

Section Two — Word Meanings

Multiple Meanings

These questions are about homographs — that's 'a word with more than one meaning' to you and me

Warm-Up Activity

1) Look at the <u>words</u> below.
2) For each word, write down <u>two different meanings</u> it may have.

      rich   ruler   match   fly   row

If you get stuck, use a <u>dictionary</u> to help you.

11+ Style Question

Take a look at this 11+ <u>sample question</u>:

> **Q** Choose the word that has a similar meaning to the words in both sets of brackets.
>
> (sphere globe) (dance party)   orb spin ball gala

- You need to pick <u>one</u> of the four options which has the <u>same meaning</u> as the <u>words in brackets</u>.
- So the answer is '<u>ball</u>' because it can mean both '<u>a sphere or globe</u>' and '<u>a dance or party</u>'.

You need to be able to recognise **Homographs** for this question

Homographs have the *Same Spelling*

<u>Homographs</u> are words that have the <u>same spelling</u> but <u>different meanings</u>:

| My watch is an hour fast. | I watch TV after dinner. |

Homographs often belong to different word types.

The word 'watch' has two different meanings in these sentences.
You only know which meaning it is by reading the rest of the sentence.

Some homographs are **Pronounced Differently**

Some homographs have the <u>same spelling</u>, but are <u>pronounced differently</u>:

| A female pig is a sow. | The farmer was going to sow his seeds. |

The word 'sow' has two different meanings in these sentences.
They're also pronounced differently, but they're both spelt the same.

Section Two — Word Meanings

Work through each word **One By One**

> **Q** Choose the word that has a similar meaning to the words in both sets of brackets.
>
> (greet salute) (sleet snow)   wave rain hail storm

Method — Rule out the wrong options

You might not recognise one of the words in brackets, but the other one will mean the same thing. Work with the word you do know.

1) <u>Read</u> through the words in the <u>brackets</u>.
2) Think about what both sets <u>mean</u>.

(greet salute) (sleet snow)   wave rain hail storm

'greet' and 'salute' mean 'to address someone'.

'sleet' and 'snow' are types of wet weather.

3) Take a look at the four options and try to <u>rule out</u> any possible answers.

'wave' can be a way of addressing someone, but it doesn't relate to wet weather — you can ignore it.

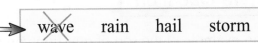

wave rain hail storm

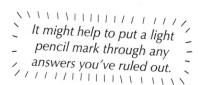

wave rain (hail) storm

It might help to put a light pencil mark through any answers you've ruled out.

'rain' and 'storm' are types of wet weather, but they don't mean 'to address or salute'. That leaves us with 'hail'.

4) <u>Double check</u> your answer by using the word in <u>two sentences</u> — one for <u>each meaning</u>.

| The weather forecast predicted hail. | ✓ |

| All hail the new king. | ✓ |

Tips and Tricks for Multiple Meanings questions

If you come across a word you don't know — don't panic! Rule out the answers that are definitely wrong. If you've got more than one possible answer left, make a sensible guess.

Practice Questions

Choose the word that has a similar meaning to the words in both sets of brackets.

1) (lecture discussion) (chat natter)   speak   talk   speech   articulate
2) (manage supervise) (sprint dash)   boss   rush   run   oversee
3) (schedule reserve) (novel text)   story   book   arrange   manual

Closest Meaning

This question type is about synonyms — that's another way of saying 'words with similar meanings'.

Warm-Up Activity

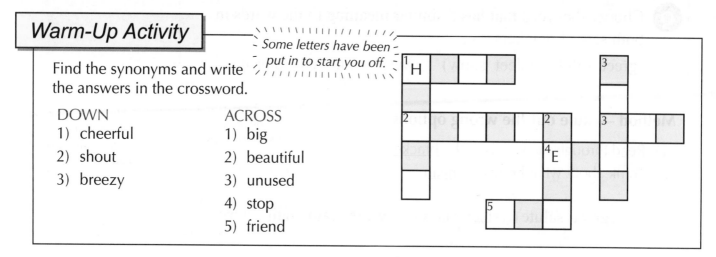

Some letters have been put in to start you off.

Find the synonyms and write the answers in the crossword.

DOWN
1) cheerful
2) shout
3) breezy

ACROSS
1) big
2) beautiful
3) unused
4) stop
5) friend

11+ Style Question

Here's an example of the sort of question you might get in the test:

> **Q** Find the word that means the same, or nearly the same, as the word on the left.
>
> **stroll**   march delay amble stride

- You need to pick the word that has the closest meaning to the word on the left.
- The answer to this question is 'amble' — like 'stroll', it means 'to walk slowly'.

You need to know about **Synonyms** to answer these questions

1) Words with similar meanings are synonyms — e.g. 'small' and 'tiny'.
2) Pairs of synonyms are usually the same word type — e.g. nouns, verbs, adjectives or adverbs.

Some questions will try to **Catch You Out**

Make sure you pick the pair of words that mean the same thing — don't just pick two words that are connected.

bucket   spade (pail) barrel cauldron

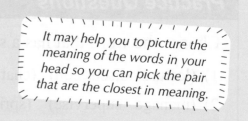

It may help you to picture the meaning of the words in your head so you can pick the pair that are the closest in meaning.

You might pick 'spade' — although it's connected to 'bucket', it doesn't mean the same thing. The right answer is 'pail'.

Use **Definitions** to help you answer the question

> **Q** Find the word that means the same, or nearly the same, as the word on the left.
>
> **stick** fused tree install club

Method 1 — Compare the meanings of words

1) Take the <u>first word</u> and think about its <u>meaning</u>.

   stick → 'stick' means 'to glue something together' or 'a piece of wood'.

   > *'stick' can be a noun or a verb. Remember to think about different word types in the test.*

2) Compare its <u>meaning</u> with each of the words on the right.

   fused → 'fused' means 'joined together' or 'fitted with a fuse'.

   The first meaning of 'fused' is about <u>joining things together</u>, just like 'stick'. But it's in the <u>past tense</u>, whereas 'stick' is in the <u>present tense</u>. So they <u>don't</u> really mean the same thing.

   tree → 'tree' means 'a large plant with a woody stem'.

   A stick comes from a tree, but they're <u>not</u> the same thing, so this isn't the answer.

   install → 'install' means 'to put something in position and connect for use'.

   'Install' is about <u>positioning</u> something, not <u>gluing</u> it, so this isn't right either.

   club → 'club' means 'a group of people with similar interests', '<u>a heavy piece of wood</u>' or 'to hit someone with a stick'.

   This definition is <u>similar</u> to something we've seen <u>before</u>...

   > *In the exam, remember to compare all the words to make sure you've found the closest match.*

   stick → 'stick' means 'to glue something together' or '<u>a piece of wood</u>'.

3) <u>'stick'</u> and <u>'club'</u> are very close in meaning — so this is the <u>answer</u>.

Tips and Tricks for Closest Meaning questions

In this question, because 'fused' is the first option, you might automatically think of the verb definition of 'stick'. That's why it's good to think about alternative definitions of the word on the left <u>before</u> you look at the options.

Section Two — Word Meanings

You can also look at **Word Type**

> **Q** Find the word that means the same, or nearly the same, as the word on the left.
>
> **rapidly**   hasty   immediate   quickly   expeditious

Method 2 — Compare the word type

Take a look back at p.16 if you're not sure about word type.

1) The correct answer will often be the <u>same type of word</u> as the word on the left — they'll both be nouns, verbs etc. — as well as having the <u>same meaning</u>.

2) Start by looking at <u>word meaning</u> and <u>rule out</u> any words that don't mean the same thing.

> **rapidly**   hasty   imme~~diate~~   quickly   expeditious

You can rule out 'immediate' because it means 'this moment', which is different from 'rapidly'. You might not know what 'expeditious' means, but don't panic — you can still work out the answer.

3) Take each word and <u>use it in a sentence</u> to help you work out the word type.

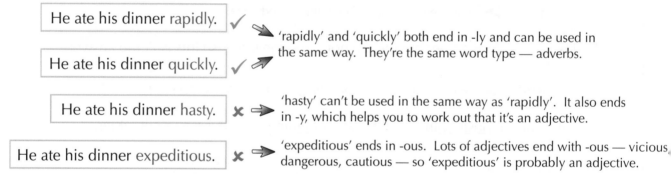

He ate his dinner rapidly. ✓

He ate his dinner quickly. ✓
'rapidly' and 'quickly' both end in -ly and can be used in the same way. They're the same word type — adverbs.

He ate his dinner hasty. ✗
'hasty' can't be used in the same way as 'rapidly'. It also ends in -y, which helps you to work out that it's an adjective.

He ate his dinner expeditious. ✗
'expeditious' ends in -ous. Lots of adjectives end with -ous — vicious, dangerous, cautious — so 'expeditious' is probably an adjective.

4) By looking at the <u>meaning</u> and the <u>word type</u>, you can work out that '<u>quickly</u>' has the <u>closest meaning</u> to '<u>rapidly</u>'.

There's **Another Type** of synonym question you might get

Here's an <u>example</u> of the sort of question you might get in the <u>test</u>:

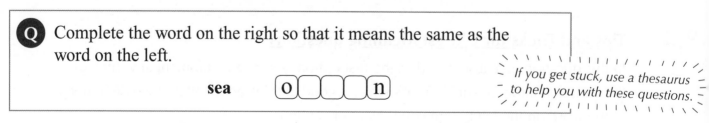

> **Q** Complete the word on the right so that it means the same as the word on the left.
>
> **sea**   [o][ ][ ][ ][n]

If you get stuck, use a thesaurus to help you with these questions.

- You need to think of a word that means the <u>same</u> as the word you're given, then write the <u>missing letters</u> in the boxes.

- A word that means the same as '<u>sea</u>' is '<u>ocean</u>', so the missing letters are '<u>c</u>', '<u>e</u>' and '<u>a</u>'.

Q Complete the word on the right so that it means the same as the word on the left.

test   ☐ h ☐ c ☐

Method — Use your knowledge of spelling patterns

1) If you can't spot the answer straight away, look at the letters you're <u>given</u> and see if you can spot any likely <u>spelling patterns</u>.

☐ h ☐ c ☐ → The second letter is 'h'. At the start of a word, 'ch', 'sh' and 'th' are all common letter patterns.

There's just one letter missing between 'h' and 'c'. These are both consonants, so it's probably a vowel. ← ☐ h ☐ c ☐

☐ h ☐ c ☐ → The second to last letter is 'c'. At the end of a word, 'ce', 'ch' and 'ck' are all common letter patterns.

2) Scribble down some words that <u>match</u> your <u>spelling patterns</u>. Think about whether any of them mean the same as the word you've been given.

thick   shock   shack   chuck   (check) → None of the others are close, but 'check' seems like it might work.

3) Try using the two words in the <u>same sentence</u> to make sure.

The doctor had to test my heart rate.

The doctor had to check my heart rate. → The two words can be used in the same way, so 'check' is the answer.

Tips and Tricks

There's a similar question type that asks you to find words with **opposite** meanings (pages 24-27), so be sure to read the instructions carefully in the test and answer the question in the right way.

Practice Questions

1) Find the word that means the same, or nearly the same, as the word on the left.

   a) **afraid**   aghast   shocked   petrified   cowardly

   b) **trail**   traipse   stride   track   tread

   c) **smiled**   sneered   grimaced   chuckled   beamed

2) Complete the word on the right so it means the same as the word on the left.

   a) **light** ☐ l ☐ ☐ ☐   b) **story** ☐ o ☐ ☐ l ☐   c) **jump** ☐ e a ☐

Opposite Meaning

The opposite of good is bad. The opposite of night is day. The opposite of synonym is antonym.

Warm-Up Activity

1) Look at the <u>words</u> below in red.
2) For <u>each word</u>, give yourself <u>30 seconds</u> to write down as <u>many words</u> as you can which mean the <u>opposite</u>. Score <u>one point</u> for each correct answer.
3) <u>Challenge</u> a friend or parent to <u>beat your score</u>.

happy   poor   serious   dainty

11+ Style Question

Here's an <u>example</u> of the sort of question you might get in the real thing:

> **Q** Find the word that means the opposite, or nearly the opposite, of the word on the left.
>
> **clean** untidy squalid dreary sterile

If you can't spot the answer straight away, start by eliminating the words that are definitely wrong.

- Pick the word that is <u>most opposite</u> in meaning to the word on the left.
- The answer is '<u>squalid</u>' because it means 'dirty', which is the opposite of '<u>clean</u>'.

This question is asking about **Antonyms**

1) Words that have <u>opposite meanings</u> are called <u>antonyms</u> — e.g. 'new' and 'old'.
2) Here are some more examples of <u>antonyms</u>:

| fat | ⇒ | skinny, slender, slim, thin |
| shout | ⇒ | mumble, murmur, mutter, whisper |

Sets of antonyms will often be the same word type.

Look at the **Prefixes**

You can turn some words into <u>antonyms</u> by adding certain <u>prefixes</u> such as <u>un-</u>, <u>dis-</u> or <u>in-</u>.

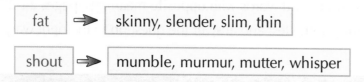 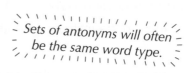

lock, tidy, friendly, well	⇒	unlock, untidy, unfriendly, unwell
appear, please, like, agree	⇒	disappear, displease, dislike, disagree
direct, edible, formal, active	⇒	indirect, inedible, informal, inactive

Use **Definitions** to help you answer the question

> **Q** Find the word that means the opposite, or nearly the opposite, of the word on the left.
>
> **frequently**   seldom   constantly   uncommon   sometimes

---

Method 1 — Compare the meanings of words ————

You can use a similar method for the opposite and closest meanings questions.

1) Take the <u>word</u> on the <u>left</u> and think about its <u>meaning</u>.

 **frequently**   seldom   constantly   uncommon   sometimes

'frequently' means 'often'.

2) Compare its <u>meaning</u> with each word on the <u>right</u>.

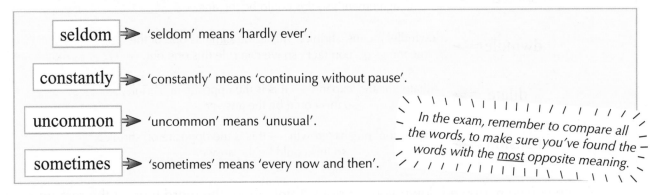

seldom ⇒ 'seldom' means 'hardly ever'.

constantly ⇒ 'constantly' means 'continuing without pause'.

uncommon ⇒ 'uncommon' means 'unusual'.

In the exam, remember to compare all the words, to make sure you've found the words with the <u>most</u> opposite meaning.

sometimes ⇒ 'sometimes' means 'every now and then'.

3) '<u>frequently</u>' means 'often', whereas '<u>seldom</u>' means 'hardly ever', so these are the <u>most opposite</u> in meaning.

4) If you have time, think of a <u>sentence</u> which uses the <u>first word</u>. Then try swapping in the <u>second word</u> to see if it makes the sentence mean the <u>opposite</u>.

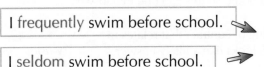

I frequently swim before school.

I seldom swim before school.

The first sentence means the opposite of the second, so 'seldom' is definitely the right answer.

<u>Tips and Tricks for Opposite Meaning questions</u>

Sometimes there might be another word that seems like a possible answer, for example 'uncommon' in the question above. This is where using the words in a sentence can help — 'I uncommon swim before school' doesn't make sense, so this **can't** be your answer.

Use **Word Type** to find the answer

> **Q** Find the word that means the opposite, or nearly the opposite, of the word on the left.
>
> **contract**   disputed   dwindle   dilate   expansion

Method 2 — Compare the word type

1) <u>Read</u> the question. <u>Think</u> about the meaning of the word on the left.

| **contract** ⟶ | 'contract' can be a <u>noun</u> meaning 'a written or spoken agreement'. It can also be a <u>verb</u> meaning 'to shrink' or 'to catch a disease'. |

2) Now <u>look</u> at the options and see if you can <u>rule any out</u> based on what they <u>mean</u>.

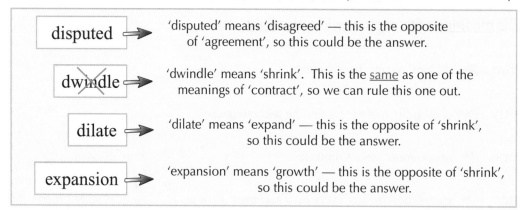

disputed ⟶	'disputed' means 'disagreed' — this is the opposite of 'agreement', so this could be the answer.
dwindle ⟶	'dwindle' means 'shrink'. This is the <u>same</u> as one of the meanings of 'contract', so we can rule this one out.
dilate ⟶	'dilate' means 'expand' — this is the opposite of 'shrink', so this could be the answer.
expansion ⟶	'expansion' means 'growth' — this is the opposite of 'shrink', so this could be the answer.

3) Once you've <u>narrowed down</u> your options, think about the <u>word type</u> of the remaining words. The answer will often be the <u>same word type</u> as the word on the left.

4) Take each word and work out its <u>word type</u>.

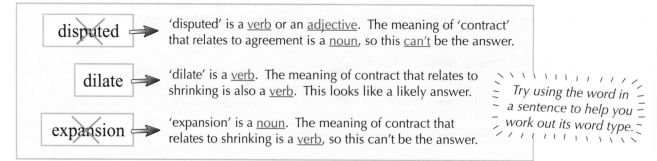

disputed ⟶	'disputed' is a <u>verb</u> or an <u>adjective</u>. The meaning of 'contract' that relates to agreement is a <u>noun</u>, so this <u>can't</u> be the answer.
dilate ⟶	'dilate' is a <u>verb</u>. The meaning of contract that relates to shrinking is also a <u>verb</u>. This looks like a likely answer.
expansion ⟶	'expansion' is a <u>noun</u>. The meaning of contract that relates to shrinking is a <u>verb</u>, so this can't be the answer.

Try using the word in a sentence to help you work out its word type.

5) By looking at the <u>meaning</u> and the <u>word type</u>, you can work out that '<u>dilate</u>' is the <u>most opposite</u> in meaning to 'contract'.

Tips and Tricks for Opposite Meaning questions

Some words belong to more than one word type, so think carefully about the different meanings of each word. Using a word in several different sentences might help.

You might also have to **Fill in the Gaps** in a word

Here's an <u>example</u> of the sort of question you might get in the <u>test</u>:

> **Q** Complete the word on the right so that it means the opposite of the word on the left.
>
> **best** ⬚⬚r⬚s⬚

Method — Check your answer carefully

1) Often, the answer to these questions will jump out at you. It's tempting to race through them, but if you're not careful you could <u>lose marks</u>.

2) <u>Before</u> you write in your answer, check that you've <u>read the question</u> properly.

best f i r s t ✗ ⟹ It's easy to misread the question and write in a word that means the same, rather than the opposite.

3) Make sure you read the <u>word you're given</u> carefully too.

best w o r s e ✗ ⟹ This answer is nearly right, but 'best' means 'most good', so you need a word that means 'most bad'. Check your answer by writing the given word in a sentence, and then trying your options in the same sentence.

It was the best day ever. → It was the worse day ever. ✗ ⟹ The first sentence doesn't make sense, but the second one does, so 'worst' is your answer.
It was the worst day ever. ✓

4) Check your <u>spelling</u> carefully, to make sure you haven't made any silly mistakes. If you're <u>not sure</u> of a spelling, writing it out a few <u>different ways</u> can help — sometimes one way will just <u>look right</u>.

⟹ | wurst | ✗ |
| werst | ✗ |
| worst | ✓ |

Practice Questions

1) Find the word that means the opposite, or nearly the opposite, of the word on the left.

   a) **present**   vacant   available   absent   blank

   b) **accuse**   preserve   defend   protect   shelter

   c) **establish**   abolish   hinder   renounce   endure

2) Complete the word on the right so it means the opposite of the word on the left.

   a) **early** ⬚l⬚⬚⬚   b) **wrong** ⬚⬚i⬚⬚t   c) **hard** ⬚⬚⬚⬚t

---

Section Two — Word Meanings

Odd One Out

The best way to prepare for Odd One Out questions is to make sure your vocabulary is top-notch...

Warm-Up Activity

1) Ask your parent or guardian to give you a <u>category</u>.
2) Try to think of as many <u>words</u> as you can that belong in that <u>category</u> — score <u>one point</u> for each word.
3) See who can get the <u>highest score</u> in your family.

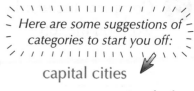

Here are some suggestions of categories to start you off:

capital cities

vegetables

animals that live in the sea

11+ Style Question

Here's an <u>example</u> of the kind of question you might get in the test:

> **Q** Three of the words in the list are linked. Mark the word that is **not** related to these three.
>
>   steal   borrow   lend   snatch

You need to pick <u>one</u> of the four words that isn't <u>connected</u> to the other three.

Method 1 — Compare the meanings of words

 1) <u>Read</u> through all the words. <u>Think</u> about what each word <u>means</u>.

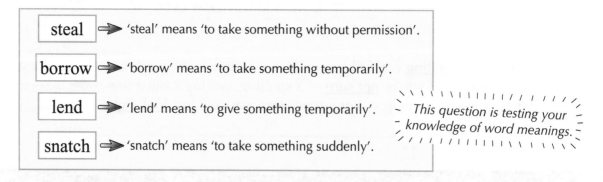

steal ⇒ 'steal' means 'to take something without permission'.

borrow ⇒ 'borrow' means 'to take something temporarily'.

lend ⇒ 'lend' means 'to give something temporarily'.

snatch ⇒ 'snatch' means 'to take something suddenly'.

This question is testing your knowledge of word meanings.

2) Try to make a <u>connection</u> between <u>three</u> of the words.

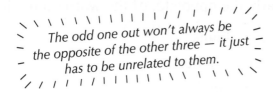

The odd one out won't always be the opposite of the other three — it just has to be unrelated to them.

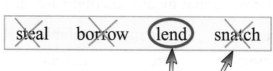

steal   borrow   (lend)   snatch

'steal', 'borrow' and 'snatch' all mean 'to take' — 'lend' means 'to give'.

3) The odd one out is '<u>lend</u>' — so that's your <u>answer</u>.

Use **Word Type** to find the answer

> **Q** Three of the words in the list are linked. Mark the word that is **not** related to these three.
>
> blemish   error   stain   mark

Method 2 — Compare the word type

1) Sometimes you might get a list of words that have <u>similar meanings</u>. To solve these questions it might help to think about <u>word type</u>.

2) <u>Read</u> through all the words. Think about the <u>word type</u> of each word.

blemish error stain mark
noun verb noun noun verb noun verb

Remember some words belong to more than one word type.

3) <u>Identify</u> any word types that <u>don't match</u> the others. Here, all four words can be <u>nouns</u> and three can be <u>verbs</u>.

4) It looks like '<u>error</u>' could be the odd one out, but have a think about what the words <u>mean</u> to make sure.

'Blemish' and 'stain' both mean 'an imperfection' or 'to make an imperfection'. 'Error' means 'something misguided or incorrect'.

'Mark' can mean 'a score' or 'to give a score', but it can also mean 'an imperfection' or 'to make an imperfection'.

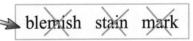

5) 'Blemish', 'stain' and 'mark' are <u>synonyms</u>, so '<u>error</u>' is the <u>odd one out</u>.

Tips and Tricks for Odd One Out questions

If you're given a group of four nouns, the question will be testing your general knowledge. Picturing each of the objects in your head may help you spot the odd one out.

Practice Questions

Three of the words in each list are linked. Mark the word that is **not** related to these three.

1) peaceful   dull   dreary   tedious
2) biography   recipe   newspaper   novel
3) lethargic   drowsy   listless   dormant
4) cheerful   morose   exultant   ecstatic

Reorder Words to Make a Sentence

Reorder the sentence in this words and halfway you're there...

Warm-Up Activity

1) Look at the <u>sentences</u> below.
2) <u>Fill</u> in the gaps with <u>sensible</u> words so that each sentence <u>makes sense</u>.

- The farmer milked his _____ in the _____.
- I _____ my pizza while I _____ my book.
- Josephine has _____ hair and _____ eyes.

11+ Style question

Here's an example of the kind of question you might be asked in the test:

> **Q** The words below can be rearranged to form a sentence.
> Mark the word that doesn't fit in the sentence.
>
> the   dinner   burned   microwave   old   heat   my

- You need to <u>rearrange</u> the words to make a <u>sentence</u> that makes sense.
- You should have one word <u>left over</u> — you need to mark this <u>word</u>.

Method 1 — Make a basic sentence

1) Make a <u>complete sentence</u> using as <u>few</u> of the words as you can.

    | the microwave burned | ⟵ This is a good start, but there
    are still quite a few words left.

    Put a light pencil mark through each word as you use it.

2) Try <u>extending</u> the sentence so it uses more words. You might need to <u>rearrange</u> it.

    | the microwave burned my dinner | ⟵ This uses most of the words. There are
    just two left — 'old' and 'heat'.

3) Try to fit one of the <u>remaining words</u> into your sentence.

    | old the microwave burned my dinner |
    | the old microwave burned my dinner | ⟵ The first sentence doesn't work, but the
    second one does. This is your sentence.

4) Check to see which word you <u>haven't used</u> in the sentence.

    'heat' is the only word that hasn't
    been used, so this is your answer. ⟹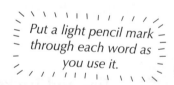

You can also look at **Sentence Structure**

Q The words below can be rearranged to form a sentence.
Mark the word that doesn't fit in the sentence.

among under troll scowled sat the and bridge the

Have a look at pages 34-37 for more on how to structure sentences.

Method 2 — Think about how sentences are formed

1) Look at the words. Sentences often start with a <u>subject</u> (i.e. the person or thing <u>doing the action</u> in the sentence). This is usually a <u>noun</u> or <u>pronoun</u> (e.g. 'I', 'he', 'she').

among under (troll) scowled sat the and (bridge) the

There are two nouns here, and no pronouns.
Try the first noun as the start of your sentence.

the troll ➡ 'troll' needs an article like 'a' or 'the' in front of it.

2) The subject is usually <u>followed</u> by a <u>verb</u>. ➡ the troll scowled / sat
There are two here — 'scowled' and 'sat'.

3) The next bit of the sentence ➡ the troll scowled / sat among / under the bridge
might tell us <u>where</u> the troll is
sitting or scowling, so look for
words that are about <u>place</u>.

The word 'bridge' is there, so that must be where the troll
is. There are two words that relate to position — 'among'
and 'under', so you need to decide which is correct.

'under the bridge' makes more ➡ the troll scowled / sat ~~among~~ / under the bridge
sense than 'among the bridge'.

4) There aren't many words left, so they should <u>slot into place</u> easily.

the troll sat under the bridge and scowled ⬅ This sentence seems to make the most sense.

5) The only word we haven't used is '<u>among</u>', so that's the <u>answer</u>.

Tips and Tricks for Reorder Words to Make a Sentence questions

It'll really help you in the test if you're familiar with how sentences are constructed —
reading lots of different books can help you get plenty of practice.

Practice Questions

The words below can be rearranged to form a sentence.
Mark the word that doesn't fit in the sentence.

1) girl know is are the I happiest Jo

2) caught walrus the into sea the and a fish rock dived

3) the if want field to quickly get there footpath take you

Preparing for Cloze Questions

'Cloze' tests are pieces of text with letters or words missing. You just have to fill in the missing bits...

You might have to **Choose** a **Whole Word**

1) In one type of cloze test, you're given some text with <u>words missing</u>. You have to choose the <u>best word</u> to fill each gap from <u>three or four options</u>.

2) Here's the type of passage you might get in the <u>test</u>:

Q Choose the correct words to complete the passage.

The answers on this page have already been filled in.

Polar bears live
☐ under
■ in
☐ with
the Arctic. They are the largest land carnivores

in the
☐ planet
☐ sea
■ world
and an adult male can weigh up to 700 kg. The number

of polar bears has
■ declined
☐ decrease
☐ risen
in recent years due to
■ hunting
☐ birth
☐ seals

and loss of sea ice.

You might have to **Fill In** missing **Letters**

1) In the <u>second type</u> of cloze test, you're given some text where some words have <u>missing letters</u>. You have to work out what the word should be, and <u>write in</u> the letters to <u>complete</u> it.

2) Here's the type of passage you might get in the <u>test</u>:

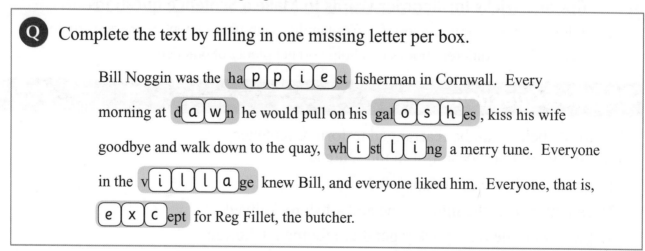

Q Complete the text by filling in one missing letter per box.

Bill Noggin was the ha p p i e st fisherman in Cornwall. Every

morning at d a w n he would pull on his gal o s h es , kiss his wife

goodbye and walk down to the quay, wh i st l i ng a merry tune. Everyone

in the v i l l a ge knew Bill, and everyone liked him. Everyone, that is,

e x c ept for Reg Fillet, the butcher.

Cloze Questions *test your* Vocabulary *and* Reading Ability...

1) The preparation you do for <u>Word Meanings</u> questions (see pages 16-31) will come in handy for <u>Cloze</u> questions too.

2) There are things you can do to <u>improve your vocabulary</u>. This will help you <u>understand</u> a piece of <u>text</u>, even when some words are missing.

- <u>Read</u> lots of different types of fiction and non-fiction texts — <u>stories</u>, <u>articles</u>, <u>poems</u> etc.
- Make a <u>list</u> of any <u>unfamiliar words</u> you come across and what they <u>mean</u>. Get a friend or family member to <u>test</u> you on your list regularly.

...*your knowledge of the* Rules *of English*...

1) In the <u>first type</u> of cloze test, there'll often be more than one option that <u>seems</u> to work, but only one of them will be <u>correct</u>. Have a look at this question:

Q The boys screamed ☐ noisy / ☐ loudly / ☐ strident when they saw the washing up.

---

2) All the options are related to making noise, but only one — '<u>loudly</u>' — is an <u>adverb</u> (a word that describes a verb, in this case 'screamed'). So this is the <u>only one</u> that <u>works</u> in the sentence.

3) You need to be able to form sentences that <u>make sense</u> and are <u>grammatically correct</u>, so you need a good knowledge of <u>grammar</u> and <u>English rules</u>. These rules are covered on pages 34-37.

4) Get lots of writing practice to help you understand how sentences are formed — write <u>letters</u> and <u>e-mails</u> to friends and relatives, as well as <u>stories</u> or <u>non-fiction texts</u> about subjects that interest you.

...*and your* Spelling

1) In the <u>second type</u> of cloze test, good <u>spelling</u> is vital.

2) Have a look at the <u>advice</u> for improving your spelling on pages 4-15, and make sure you know your <u>spelling patterns</u> inside out.

Practice Questions

1) Choose the correct word from the options in **bold** to complete each sentence.
   a) It was getting **dark** / **sunny** / **quiet**, so I turned on the light.
   b) Harry fell off the camel and **jumped** / **crawled** / **landed** on his feet.
   c) Playing basketball **enlarges** / **accelerates** / **improves** your coordination.

2) Complete each sentence by filling in one missing letter per box.
   a) Chen and Beth ran away from the ☐☐ly monster.
   b) I go swimming with my ☐rie☐☐s every Monday night.
   c) My dog won't stop scratching — I think he has ☐l☐☐s.

Using Rules of English — Verbs

Having a good grasp of English rules and how sentences are put together will help with cloze questions. Luckily, the next few pages tell you what you need to know.

A *Sentence Always* has a *Verb*

Verbs can also be 'being' words, e.g. in the sentence 'I am cold', the verb is 'am'.

1) Verbs are <u>action</u> words — they describe what the <u>subject</u> of the sentence is <u>doing</u>.

'Andy' is the subject because he is 'doing' the action. → | Andy baked a cake. | ← 'baked' is the verb.

| Running is good for your health. | ← 'Running' is the subject because the verb 'is' describes what the subject does.

2) The subject and verb <u>have to agree</u>. This just means that a <u>singular subject</u> needs a <u>singular form</u> of the verb, and a <u>plural subject</u> needs a <u>plural form</u> of the verb.

| Majid is in the car. |

The subject is 'Majid'. It's singular, as there's only one person.
The verb is 'is'. It's singular too.

| Majid and Neha are in the car. |

The subject here is 'Majid and Neha' — there's more than one person, so it's plural.
The verb 'are' is also plural, to match the subject.

Phrases and *Clauses Add Information* to a *Sentence*

<u>Phrases</u> and <u>clauses</u> are groups of words that are used to form sentences.

A *Phrase Doesn't* have a *Verb...*

A phrase <u>doesn't</u> contain a verb.

| Jade wore her new purple dress. | ← 'her new purple dress' is a phrase.

...But a *Clause Does*

A clause is the same as a phrase — except that it <u>contains</u> a verb.

| Suzy listened to the radio while she brushed her teeth. | ⇐ This is a clause. The verb is 'brushed'.

The *Tense* of a verb tells you *When It's Happening*

Verbs can be in the <u>past</u> tense, the <u>present</u> tense or the <u>future</u> tense.

| Roberta played the lead role. | ⇐ past tense ⇒ | Roberta has played the lead role. |

| Roberta plays the lead role. | ⇐ present tense ⇒ | Roberta is playing the lead role. |

| Roberta will play the lead role. | ⇐ future tense ⇒ | Roberta will be playing the lead role. |

Sometimes there's more than one verb together in a sentence.

Make sure that you can **Use Verbs** in the **Correct Tense**

> **Q** In each sentence, one verb has been used incorrectly.
> Rewrite the sentences using the correct form of the verb.
>
> a) *"Quick, everyone went to your lookouts!" ordered the fireman.*
> b) *The ball was kick into the back of the net.*
> c) *My rabbit is escape at this very moment.*
> d) *Yesterday, my brother refuse to clean his bedroom.*

Method — Work out when the action is happening

1) Read the <u>first sentence</u> and work out which verb is <u>wrong</u>.

a) "Quick, everyone went to your lookouts!" ordered the fireman.

This doesn't sound right. The fireman is issuing an instruction in the present tense, and 'went' is in the past tense.

a) "Quick, everyone go to your lookouts!" ordered the fireman. ← This is better. The past tense 'went' has changed to the present tense, 'go'.

2) Do the <u>same</u> for the rest of the sentences:

b) The ball was kicked into the back of the net. ← The clue here is 'was' — it tells you that the sentence is in the past tense. So you need to change 'kick' to 'kicked'.

c) My rabbit is escaping at this very moment. ← 'is' tells you that this sentence is in the present tense and it's still happening. So you need to change 'escape' to 'escaping'.

d) Yesterday, my brother refused to clean his bedroom. ← The word 'Yesterday' tells you that the sentence is in the past tense. So use 'refused' instead of 'refuse'.

Tips and Tricks for Choosing Verbs

Look at the words around the verb to help you work out the tense

of the sentence and who is doing the action.

Practice Questions

1) Circle the correct verb to complete each sentence.
   a) Barney has *eating / eat / eaten* all of my popcorn.
   b) I have *going / been / went* to South Africa on holiday.
   c) Barry's knee is *hurted / hurts / hurting* after he fell over.
   d) You should *got / go / went* home or you'll be late.
   e) What time do you think you will *arriving / arrive / arrived*?
   f) The dolphin is about to *leaps / leaping / leap* out of the water.

Using Rules of English — Connectives

Connectives are like glue — they join different parts of a text together.

Connectives Join Clauses and Sentences

1) Connectives join <u>clauses</u> together in a <u>sentence</u>.

| I haven't got my homework because my dog ate it. |

| It was raining so Mohammed put up his umbrella. |

2) Connectives can also link <u>sentences</u> together in a <u>text</u>.

| The plans for the town centre gardens will certainly bring more tourists to the town. On the other hand, more tourists will mean an increase in traffic coming into town. Furthermore, the new gardens will cost the council a lot of money. |

'On the other hand' introduces a different point of view.

'Furthermore' adds to this point of view.

You'll see connectives used like this a lot in letters and newspaper articles.

Connectives can be Words or Short Phrases

Connectives may be Short Words

These short words are also called 'conjunctions'.

These are words like '<u>so</u>', '<u>if</u>', '<u>and</u>', '<u>but</u>', '<u>while</u>' and '<u>since</u>'.

| Mum's going to do some baking and she would like you to help. |

| Let's go for a walk today while the weather is nice. |

Connectives may be Compound Words

1) <u>Compound words</u> are made from two smaller words <u>joined together</u>.
2) These are words like '<u>however</u>', '<u>moreover</u>', '<u>whereas</u>' and '<u>meanwhile</u>'.

| Julie wanted to go to the shops, whereas I wanted to go swimming. However, the swimming pool was closed, so our decision was made for us. |

Connectives may be Short Phrases

These are phrases like '<u>as soon as</u>', '<u>on the other hand</u>', '<u>in other words</u>' and '<u>as a result</u>'.

| Wally wasn't sure where the exit was. In other words, he was lost. |

| Nadine had left her homework at home. As a result, her teacher put her in detention. |

You need to **Know How to Use Connectives**

 Q Circle the most appropriate connective to complete each sentence.

a) Jack's new puppy was a bundle of energy *because / but / furthermore / so*
it certainly wasn't house-trained.

b) My bus was late again today *although / therefore / also / because*
the driver had called in sick.

c) I'm really looking forward to the disco tonight *because / so / although / in case*
I don't know what to wear.

Method — Look for the meaning of the sentence

1) Look for the <u>relationship</u> between the <u>two clauses</u> in each sentence.
This gives the sentence its <u>meaning</u>.

2) Choose the <u>connective</u> to fit the meaning of the sentence.

a) Jack's new puppy was a bundle of energy but it certainly wasn't house-trained.

The first clause gives a positive description of Jack's new puppy... ... whilst the second clause introduces a negative point. So 'but' is the most logical connective to use.

b) My bus was late again today because the driver had called in sick.

The first clause explains that the bus was late... ... and the second clause explains why. So use 'because' to introduce the explanation.

c) I'm really looking forward to the disco tonight although I don't know what to wear.

The first clause is a positive statement... ... but the second clause makes a negative point. 'although' is the most logical connective to use.

Practice Questions

1) Underline the connectives in the passage below.

*The Amazon Rainforest covers 40% of South America, although it has decreased
in size. Humans have cut down the trees because they need wood for construction
and space to build farms. However, conservation efforts are under way
to protect the rainforest and stop people from illegally cutting down the trees.*

2) Circle the most appropriate connective to complete each sentence.

a) I like to eat cereal for breakfast. *Consequently, / As a result, / Therefore, / However,*
I sometimes eat a slice of toast.

b) I'd like to go out to the Italian restaurant tonight, *although / therefore / because / so*
Chinese is my favourite.

c) We went to play hockey, *whenever / although / despite / until* the rain.

Answering Cloze Questions

Once your vocab is top-notch and you've got a sound knowledge of grammar, cloze tests should be a breeze. But just in case you want a bit of extra guidance, here are some methods for completing them...

Work Out *what the passage is* About First

> **Q** Choose the correct words to complete the passage.
>
> Of all the ☐ moons / ☐ stars / ☐ planets in the solar system, Mercury is the ☐ closest / ☐ close / ☐ closer to the
>
> Sun. As a result, its surface ☐ getting / ☐ got / ☐ gets extremely hot during the day.
>
> ☐ Considering / ☐ Despite / ☐ Without these high temperatures, scientists ☐ pretend / ☐ believe / ☐ assume that ice
>
> exists on Mercury, just as it does on Earth.

Method 1 — Look at the context of each missing word

As you read, try not to look at the options, but think for yourself what the right answers might be.

1) Have a quick skim through the <u>whole text</u> first — this will help you work out <u>what it's about</u>, which makes it much easier to find the right answers.

2) Now look at the <u>first question</u>. Don't just look at the options — look at the <u>whole sentence</u>.

> Of all the ☐ moons / ☐ stars / ☐ planets in the solar system,

There's only one star in the solar system, so you can rule that out, but either 'moons' or 'planets' could be correct.

> Mercury is the ☐ closest / ☐ close / ☐ closer to the Sun.

But when you read the rest of the sentence, it's talking about Mercury — a planet in our solar system.

3) So the answer to the first question is '<u>planets</u>'.

☐ moons / ☐ stars / ■ planets

4) You can use the <u>same method</u> to work out the <u>second answer</u>. The start of the sentence compares Mercury to '<u>all</u> the planets', so you know it must be the <u>most close</u>. The word for this is '<u>closest</u>', so that's your answer.

■ closest / ☐ close / ☐ closer

Use your **Knowledge** of **Grammar**

Method 2 — Think about rules of English

1) For the next question you have to choose the <u>right form</u> of the <u>verb</u> 'to get'.

2) Read the <u>whole sentence</u> to work out whether it's in the <u>past</u>, <u>present</u> or <u>future</u> tense.

As a result, its surface ☐ getting ☐ got ☐ gets extremely hot during the day.

From the sentence alone, you can't tell what tense it should be in. You need to look for clues in the rest of the text.

3) Look for <u>other verbs</u> in the passage. → exists is

These are in the present tense, so our missing verb must be too.

☐ getting
☐ got
■ gets

4) 'getting' is only <u>part</u> of the verb — it would need 'is' in front of it to make it present tense. 'got' is past tense, so the <u>answer</u> is '<u>gets</u>'.

It might help to answer the questions **Out of Order**

Method 3 — Work out the meaning of the sentence

1) Look at the <u>next question</u>.

☐ Considering
☐ Despite   these high temperatures, scientists...
☐ Without

This is a tricky one because you don't get many clues from this part of the sentence. Any of these options could work.

2) Before you can work out this answer, you need to work out the <u>next answer</u> so you <u>understand</u> the <u>full sentence</u>.

...scientists ☐ pretend ☐ believe   that ice exists on Mercury... ☐ assume

Scientists come up with theories and back them up with evidence — they don't usually pretend or assume things.

3) You've <u>ruled out</u> 'pretend' and 'assume', so the answer must be '<u>believe</u>'. Now that you know this, <u>look back</u> at the first part of the sentence.

☐ Considering
☐ Despite   these high temperatures, scientists
☐ Without
☐ pretend
■ believe   that ice exists...
☐ assume

4) The sentence says that Mercury is <u>hot</u>, but there's <u>ice</u> there, so you're looking for a word that shows a <u>contradiction</u>. The answer is '<u>Despite</u>'. →

☐ Considering
■ Despite
☐ Without

Check your **Spelling** carefully in cloze tests with **Missing Letters**

> **Q** Complete the text by filling in one missing letter per box.
>
> Although pirates are frequently portrayed as immoral and dis☐☐☐est , pirate ships were of☐☐n run democratically. The captain and quartermaster were el☐☐☐ed by the crew, and any plunder seized during at☐☐☐ks on other ships was shared amongst all the sa☐☐☐rs .

Method 1 — Think about word type and meaning

1) Read through the <u>whole text</u> first and try to get an idea of what it's about.

2) Now look at the <u>first incomplete word</u> and how it fits into the sentence.

> Although pirates are frequently portrayed as immoral and dis☐☐☐est ...

> The sentence is talking about how pirates are seen, so it's probably an adjective. The word 'immoral' is negative and the connective 'and' is used, so the missing word is probably negative too.

3) Run through some <u>negative adjectives</u> that start with '<u>dis</u>' to see if any of them <u>fit</u> with the sentence.

> dishonest

This makes sense and fits with the letters you're given. So you need to write '<u>hon</u>' in the boxes.

4) Move on to the <u>remaining words</u> and look at how they <u>fit into their sentences</u>.

> ...pirate ships were of☐☐n run democratically.

The sentence starts with 'Although', so you know it will contradict the view that pirates were immoral. A word like 'usually' would make sense here — 'often' means the same and fits with the letters you're given, so you need to fill in '<u>te</u>'.

The missing word says what was done by the crew, so it must be a verb. Looking at the sentence before, it's probably connected to democracy, so 'elected' seems like a good choice. Write in '<u>ect</u>'.

> The captain and quartermaster were el☐☐☐ed by the crew

Method 2 — Write out the full word

1) You'll often spot the answer <u>quickly</u>, but it can still be <u>tricky</u> to fill in the right letters.

This word is 'attacks', but when you're working quickly it's easy to make a mistake.

> ...plunder seized during at☐☐☐ks...

at☐t☐☐t☐a☐ks ✗   at☐a☐☐c☐c☐ks ✗   at☐t☐☐a☐c☐ks ✓

2) Write out the <u>full word</u> on some scrap paper <u>before</u> you fill in the missing letters — it'll make it much easier to <u>spot any mistakes</u>.

> ...shared amongst all the sa☐☐☐rs .

salers ✗   saliors ✗
sailers ✗   sailors ✓ → sa☐i☐☐l☐o☐rs

Practice Questions

1) Choose the correct words to complete the passage.

At
☐ more
☐ down
☐ up
to thirty metres long, blue whales are
☐ approximately
☐ definitely
☐ usually
three times the

☐ weight
☐ length
☐ height
of a double-decker bus. These
☐ massively
☐ diminutive
☐ colossal
marine mammals eat four

to eight tonnes of krill, tiny sea creatures,
☐ one
☐ every
☐ all
day. Blue whales have a fringe of fine

plates
☐ associated
☐ detached
☐ attached
to their upper jaw. To feed, they
☐ take
☐ took
☐ taken
in a huge mouthful

of water and force it out
☐ between
☐ through
☐ beyond
the fringe. The krill are too
☐ tiny
☐ big
☐ clever
to pass

between the plates,
☐ so
☐ providing
☐ then
they stay in the whale's mouth.

2) Complete the text by filling in one missing letter per box.

With a groan, the sol☐☐☐r came to. His head felt as th☐☐☐h someone had

been using it as a football. With a grunt of p☐☐n, he scrambled to his feet and

wa☐☐☐d for the sky to stop its alarming spinning. He bent slowly and picked up

his rifle, then stumbled o☐w☐rd. His inj☐☐☐d ankle made it difficult to walk

quickly, but he knew he had to reach the tr☐☐ch before the next round of shelling

st☐☐t☐d. He was so close — he could almost reach out and touch the bank of

ea☐☐☐ that marked the edge of the ditch. Just a few more paces and he would reach

safety and s☐☐☐☐er.

Reading the Text

Comprehension texts come in all shapes and sizes — here's how to tackle them...

Warm-Up Activity

1) Find an unwanted <u>magazine</u> and <u>newspaper</u>.
2) <u>Cut</u> out an <u>article</u> from each of them.
3) For both articles, write down a <u>key word</u> which sums up each paragraph.

Texts can be **Divided** into **Fiction** and **Non-fiction**

1) <u>Fiction</u> texts are <u>made up</u> by the author, and are about <u>imaginary events</u> and <u>people</u>. <u>Non-fiction</u> texts are based on <u>facts</u>, and are about <u>real people</u> and <u>events</u>.

2) Here are some <u>examples</u> of the types of texts you might get in your reading comprehension:

Fiction Texts

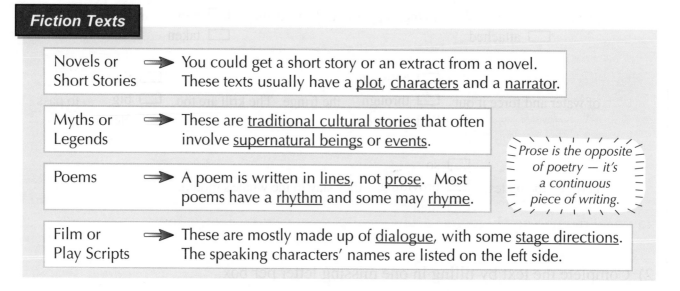

| Novels or Short Stories | ➤ You could get a short story or an extract from a novel. These texts usually have a <u>plot</u>, <u>characters</u> and a <u>narrator</u>. |

| Myths or Legends | ➤ These are <u>traditional cultural stories</u> that often involve <u>supernatural beings</u> or <u>events</u>. |

Prose is the opposite of poetry — it's a continuous piece of writing.

| Poems | ➤ A poem is written in <u>lines</u>, not <u>prose</u>. Most poems have a <u>rhythm</u> and some may <u>rhyme</u>. |

| Film or Play Scripts | ➤ These are mostly made up of <u>dialogue</u>, with some <u>stage directions</u>. The speaking characters' names are listed on the left side. |

Non-fiction Texts

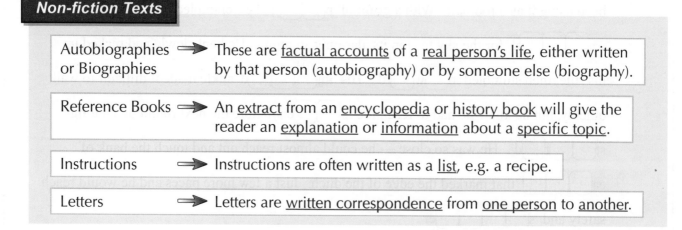

| Autobiographies or Biographies | ➤ These are <u>factual accounts</u> of a <u>real person's life</u>, either written by that person (autobiography) or by someone else (biography). |

| Reference Books | ➤ An <u>extract</u> from an <u>encyclopedia</u> or <u>history book</u> will give the reader an <u>explanation</u> or <u>information</u> about a <u>specific topic</u>. |

| Instructions | ➤ Instructions are often written as a <u>list</u>, e.g. a recipe. |

| Letters | ➤ Letters are <u>written correspondence</u> from <u>one person</u> to <u>another</u>. |

Comprehension Questions *ask you to* Pick Out Details

You can use this <u>method</u> to tackle <u>comprehension questions</u> in the test.

Make sure that your highlighting doesn't slow down your reading too much.

Method — Highlight key words

1) As you read, <u>scan</u> the text looking for <u>information</u> which gives you the <u>main points</u> of the text, and <u>highlight</u> a few <u>key words</u>.

2) <u>Key words</u> are things that tell you <u>who</u>, <u>what</u>, <u>where</u>, <u>when</u>, <u>why</u> and <u>how</u>.

This tells you what the passage is about. ⟹

Not much is known about the origins of Stonehenge. Nobody knows when it was erected, but most historians think that it must have happened between 3000 and 2000 BC. Equally, it is unclear why it was built; some scholars argue that it served a religious purpose, but others think that it was a kind of observatory, to study the movements of the stars and planets.

These dates would be helpful in a 'when' question.

These purposes would be helpful in a 'why' question.

3) Read the <u>questions</u>, using the <u>key words</u> that you've <u>highlighted</u> as <u>signposts</u> to help you find <u>where</u> the <u>important information</u> is in the text.

This question asks 'when', so you need to look for dates.

Q 1) When does the text suggest Stonehenge was built?

2) What reasons does the text give for its construction?

This question asks 'what reasons', so you need to look for purposes.

Practice Questions

1) Read the passage below and then answer the questions that follow.

1 *Joaquin couldn't believe his eyes. Standing in front of him was Eric Debuski,*
2 *lead vocalist of the 'Island Sandmen'. Eric, otherwise known as Lavahead, wasn't*
3 *wearing his trademark deerhunter and aviators, but there was no doubt about it.*
4 *It was him all right! Joaquin had worked here for two whole years and this was the*
5 *most exciting thing that had happened in all that time. He'd never met anyone famous*
6 *before, and now he was meeting the frontman of his favourite band. It was astounding.*
7 *"Hey kid," Eric said commandingly, "you might want to try shutting that mouth."*
8 *Joaquin swallowed loudly. "S-S-Sorry", he stammered, as he scanned through Eric's*
9 *basket. Eric just stood back and gazed lazily, almost as if he were a normal person.*

a) What is Eric Debuski's stage name?

b) What word in the passage can mean the same as 'lead vocalist' (line 2)?

c) What kind of place does Joaquin work in?

d) Why do you think Eric tells Joaquin to shut his mouth?

e) What evidence is there in the passage to suggest how Joaquin was feeling?

Understanding the Questions

Here are some lovely pages about 'Understanding the Questions'— just my cup of tea.

Make sure you Learn the Different Question Types

1) You need to use <u>different skills</u> for different <u>question types</u>.

2) <u>Learn</u> to recognise question types so you know <u>how</u> to <u>answer</u> them.

The same question types come up in both standard answer and multiple choice tests. See p.58-59 for more about the two question styles.

Fact Finding Questions

Fact finding questions usually use words like <u>who</u>, <u>where</u>, <u>what</u>, <u>when</u>, <u>why</u> and <u>how</u>:

What are the names of the two brothers?
When did the ship set sail?

You should be able to find answers to these questions simply by reading through the passage carefully.

— Method — Find the facts

1) First, you need to look at the <u>question</u> to find out <u>what</u> you are <u>looking for</u>. You may need to read between the lines if the answer is <u>not obvious</u>.

Who is George's oldest son?

'Who' tells you that you're looking for a name.
'oldest' tells you to look for information about ages.

See p.46-47 for more advice on tricky find the facts questions

2) Scan the text for the <u>information</u> that will help you <u>work out</u> the answer.

Buster is the youngest, so it can't be him.

George had four sons: Mike, Oscar, Toby and Buster. As the youngest, Buster was spoiled growing up, whilst Mike and Toby competed over who was the favourite middle child.

The oldest must be one of these four.

Mike and Toby are the middle children, so it can't be them.

3) This information shows that <u>Oscar</u> must be the <u>oldest son</u>.

Questions about Word Meanings

You might need to use your knowledge of <u>word meanings</u> to answer a question:

How did Cody feel about the state of the kitchen?

The key words in the question tell you what it is asking.

— Method — Think about word meanings

1) Once you know what the question is <u>asking</u>, you can <u>find</u> the <u>information</u> in the text:

Cody was repulsed by what he saw in the kitchen.

The text tells you how he feels.

2) If the question gives you options, <u>choose</u> the one that has the <u>closest meaning</u>:

A He was delighted.
B He was appalled.
C He was disgusted.
D He was confused.

Out of all the options 'disgusted' is the closest to 'repulsed', so C is the answer.

See p.48-49 for more advice on questions about word meaning.

Multiple-Statement Questions

You may be given a <u>list</u> of <u>statements</u> and asked which ones are <u>right</u> or <u>wrong</u>.

Method — Narrow down the options

According to the text who were the last two Conservative prime ministers?

1. Margaret Thatcher   2. Tony Blair

3. David Cameron   4. John Major

A 1 and 2
B 2 and 3
C 2 and 4 ← You need to pick out the letter which matches
D 3 and 4   the correct combination of options.

Some multiple statement questions just ask for one answer, e.g. 'Which of these statements is true?'

You need to work out which <u>two options</u> are correct, using <u>information</u> from the text.

> The Conservative Party dominated British politics during the 1980s and early 1990s. Margaret Thatcher was Prime Minister from 1979 to 1990, followed by John Major from 1990 to 1997. After that, the Labour Party regained power with the election of Tony Blair. They remained in power led by Gordon Brown until 2010 when the Conservatives won the vote and David Cameron came to office.

Here's one of the answers...

...and here's the other answer. So you need the letter which matches option 3 and 4 — letter D.

You'll need to use <u>logic</u> to answer some multiple-statement questions — see pages 53-55.

Reasoning Questions

You might need to use common sense to work out the answers to some reasoning questions.

Reasoning questions ask about the text's <u>purpose</u> or <u>meaning</u>.

1) These questions could use phrases like '<u>most likely</u>' or ask you about the <u>opinions</u> of the <u>author</u> or <u>characters</u>.

These questions are asking about the passage's purpose. ⇒

What is the writer's view of wine in general?
Where would you be most likely to read this passage?

2) Questions that ask '<u>why</u>' or '<u>what do you think</u>' might test your own <u>opinion</u>. <u>Think about</u> the <u>impression</u> you get from the text's <u>language</u> and <u>tone</u>.

If a question asks you about something that isn't in the text, look for clues in the information you've been given.

Why does Amir keep his prize a secret?
How do you think Tom felt when he was caught?

For questions like this, think about how you would feel in the character's place.

Section Four — Comprehension

Finding Hidden Facts

Some comprehension questions test your detective skills — you'll need to read very carefully.

Sometimes you'll have to Count Up Facts

> **Q** Read the passage and then answer the questions that follow.
>
> *Five children - Harry, Farooq, Dimitri, Emma and Sophie - are talking about their families and pets. Harry has two sisters and a brother. The girls are both only-children, but Sophie has her pet cat, Tiger, to keep her company. Dimitri and Harry each have a dog, and everyone except Sophie has a pet fish. Farooq says he would like a cat, but his brother is allergic to them. Dimitri has two sisters and a hamster.*
>
> 1. How many of the children have a brother? _____
>
> 2. Who has the most pets? _____

Method — Make a table when it helps

1) Read the <u>first question</u> carefully. You can <u>ignore</u> the second question for now.

2) Read all the information you're given, <u>picking out</u> the facts you need to answer the first question — which children have a <u>brother</u>.

> *Harry has two sisters (and a brother.)*
> *Farooq says he would like a cat, but (his brother) is allergic to them.*

Harry and Farooq each have a brother, so the <u>answer</u> is <u>two</u>.

3) Now move on to the <u>second question</u>. A <u>tally chart</u> will help you here.

4) Write down everyone's initial, then put <u>marks</u> next to each initial for the <u>pets</u> that person has.

5) Watch out for <u>confusing information</u> — Farooq <u>would like</u> a cat, but he <u>doesn't</u> have one.

6) <u>Read off</u> the <u>table</u> to answer the question. You're looking for the person who has the <u>most marks</u> next to their <u>initial</u>.

7) The answer is <u>Dimitri</u>.

Initials of people

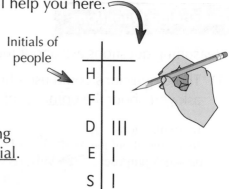

H	II
F	I
D	III
E	I
S	I

Some phrases can catch you out

You need to look out for <u>phrases</u> like these:

| 'All the children...' | 'All the boys...' | 'All the girls...' | '...apart from...' |

| 'Kieran did not...' | 'Everyone except...' | 'The only one who...' |

You might have to work out **How Long** something took

Q Read the passage and then answer the question that follows.

Max and Jade had always dreamt of having a tree house at the bottom of their garden. One Friday, after school, they decided to start building one themselves.

Their father agreed to help them with the work. He was a carpenter, and every day he helped his children to build a strong, safe tree house.

Max and Jade worked tirelessly all weekend, and by Monday they had a basic frame. After three more days of hard work, their tree house was finally complete.

All that was left to do was to celebrate their achievement. They prepared a feast of sandwiches, crisps and cakes, and invited their dad as the guest of honour.

How many days did it take Max and Jade to build the tree house? _____

Method — Pick out the important bits of information

1) Read all the information you're given, and <u>pick out</u> the bits that are about <u>time</u>.

> *One Friday, after school, they decided to start building...*

They started on a Friday.

> *...every day he helped...*

This one's about time, but it doesn't really tell us anything.

> *...and by Monday...*

They were still digging on Monday.

> *After three more days of hard work, their tree house was finally complete.*

They finished on Thursday — three days after Monday.

2) So they started on Friday and finished on Thursday — that's <u>seven days</u>.

Practice Question

Read the passage, then answer the questions that follow.

Glen, Ali, Kim, Marta and Luca are looking out of the windows of the school bus. Glen and Marta see a pedestrian and a cat. Kim, Ali and Luca see a yellow car. Marta and Ali see a tractor. Everyone except Kim sees a cyclist.

1. Who sees the most things? _____

2. How many children see a motorised vehicle? _____

Section Four — Comprehension

Word Meanings

Knowing lots of words will help you in the test. Luckily, learning new words doesn't have to be boring.

Reading will **Improve** your **Vocabulary**

If you've read Section 2, you'll already have some ideas of fun ways to improve your vocabulary (all the words you know). In case you nodded off for a minute, here's a quick recap...

1) Read lots of different things — novels, newspapers and magazines.
2) If you come across a word you don't know, look it up in a dictionary and write down what it means.
3) Do crosswords and other word games.

Have a look back at page 16 for more details.

If you come across a word you don't know in the test, don't panic.
There are some tricks you can use to help you work out what it means.

You might be asked what a word **Means**

> **Q** Read the passage and then answer the questions that follow.
>
> *The owl sat upon the bridge feeling disgruntled, staring down at her reflection in the water below. Only that morning she had been the wisest owl in the forest, but that accolade had been taken by her ecstatic sister. Her eyes suddenly focused on the pool below as a small face broke the surface.*
>
> 1. What does the word 'disgruntled' mean?
>   **A** Surprised
>   **B** Annoyed
>   **C** Bored
>   **D** Confused

Method 1 — Look at the rest of the passage for clues

1) Look at the context of the word for clues about what it means.

> *The owl sat upon the bridge feeling disgruntled... Only that morning she had been the wisest owl in the forest, but that accolade had been taken...*

The owl used to be the wisest, but she isn't any more. This is likely to make her feel upset or offended.

2) Look through the options for a word that means 'upset' or 'offended'.

> **A** Surprised ✗
> **B** Annoyed ✓
> **C** Bored ✗
> **D** Confused ✗

'annoyed' is the only option that has a similar meaning to 'upset', so that's the answer.

Q 2. What does the word 'accolade' mean?

    A Punishment

    B Joyful

    C Trophy

    D Honour

Method 2 — Use word type to narrow down the options

1) Look at the <u>context</u> of the word and work out what <u>type</u> of word it is.

> It's something that has been taken, so it must be a noun. The thing that has been taken is the position of wisest owl — this isn't a physical thing that you can see or touch, so it must be an abstract noun.

> *...she had been the wisest owl in the forest, but that accolade had been taken by her ecstatic sister...*

2) Narrow down the options by <u>ruling out</u> words that <u>aren't abstract nouns</u>.

    A Punishment

    B Joyful ✗

    C Trophy ✗

    D Honour

> 'Joyful' is an adjective, and 'trophy' is a common noun. 'Punishment' and 'honour' can both be abstract nouns, so you need to think about what they mean.

3) The text tells you that the 'accolade' is the position of wisest owl. This is a <u>good thing</u>, so 'punishment' <u>doesn't make sense</u>. The answer must be '<u>honour</u>'.

Tips and Tricks for Word Meaning Questions

These methods can often help you to work out the answer, but sometimes you just have to know the word. So with these questions you need to remember the golden rule of multiple choice — if you don't know the answer, guess.

Practice Questions

Read the passage below and then answer the questions that follow.

Laura glanced down at the ground far below her and gulped. Mrs Parry had pleaded so fervently for her help that she hadn't felt able to refuse. But now, with the ladder wobbling alarmingly, she was starting to regret her benevolence. Next time, she thought grimly, she'd be more circumspect about offering to rescue cats from trees.

1) What does the word 'fervently' mean?

    A Emotionally   **B** Calmly   **C** Angrily   **D** Joyfully

2) What does the word 'circumspect' mean?

    A Forethought   **B** Anxiety   **C** Enthusiastic   **D** Cautious

Understanding the Language in the Text

Imagery is just a fancy word for writing that creates a picture in your mind.

Figurative Language gives you a Picture

1) <u>Literal language</u> means <u>exactly</u> what it says.

Dave is a real clown. ← If you are talking about someone called Dave who works as a clown, then this is a literal statement.

2) <u>Figurative language</u> doesn't mean exactly what it says.

Dave is a real clown. ← If you're describing someone who jokes around a lot but who isn't actually a clown, then this is a figurative statement.

3) <u>Imagery</u> is a type of <u>figurative language</u> — it's <u>language</u> that is used to give the reader a <u>vivid picture</u> of something.

The field of tulips I saw from the window was like a red carpet stretching into the distance.

This imagery makes you imagine a red carpet, and this shows you what the field of tulips was like.

The pie was as fragrant as a rotten egg, and its crust was concrete.

This imagery helps you to imagine how bad the pie smelt...

... and this imagery tells you how hard the crust was, but you know it isn't actually made of concrete.

There are lots of different types of Imagery

A Simile says that One Thing is Like Another

1) A <u>simile</u> describes something by <u>comparing it</u> to something else.
2) Similes always use a <u>comparing word</u> like '<u>as</u>' or '<u>like</u>'.

His anger erupted like a volcano. The simile helps you to imagine the force of his anger.

Jackie's cheeks were as white as snow. This simile emphasises how white Jackie's cheeks were.

Life is like a rollercoaster. Life is being compared to a rollercoaster in this simile.

A *Metaphor* says that *One Thing Is Another*

1) A <u>metaphor</u> describes something as <u>actually being</u> something else.

2) It's an example of <u>figurative writing</u>.

> Jack's eyes were deep black oily pools. ← This gives a vivid description of Jack's eyes, but they're not actually deep black oily pools.

> The living room was a furnace. ← The living room wasn't actually a furnace, but the metaphor shows that the room was very hot.

Personification describes a *Thing* as a *Person*

> *Personification makes descriptions come to life.*

<u>Personification</u> describes something that's not human as if it is a <u>person</u>.

> The sea races up the beach. ← This sounds like the sea has the ability to run.

> The sun smiled on the shoppers below. ← This sounds like the sun has a human expression.

> Time had been kind to Raj; there was not a wrinkle on his face. ← This sounds like time was deliberately nice to Raj.

Irony is often used to *Create Humour*

Verbal Irony is where the *Opposite Meaning* is meant

1) <u>Verbal irony</u> is where the writer means the <u>opposite</u> to what they have <u>actually written</u>.

2) You can usually tell that the writer is being ironic from the <u>context</u> of the writing.

> We were stranded at the airport for 48 hours with no food, which was just great.

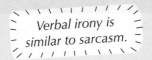

> *Verbal irony is similar to sarcasm.*

The writer doesn't actually mean that it was great — they actually mean the opposite. This is irony.

Situational Irony is where *Unexpected Events Occur*

<u>Situational irony</u> is where the <u>opposite</u> thing happens to what the reader <u>expects</u>.

> While the two robbers were robbing the bank, someone stole their car.

We don't expect someone to steal from the robbers. This is an example of situational irony — it is the opposite of what we expect to happen.

You might have to **Work Out** what **Figurative Language** means

> **Q** Read the passage and then answer the questions that follow.
>
> *I set off by the early morning coach before it was yet light, and was out on the open country road when the day came creeping on, halting and whimpering and shivering, and wrapped in patches of cloud and rags of mist, like a beggar.*
>
> **From 'Great Expectations' by Charles Dickens**
>
> What is meant by the phrase 'the day came creeping on'?
> **A** The narrator was trying to move quietly.
> **B** The narrator was being followed by a beggar.
> **C** The early morning light was spooky.
> **D** It got light very gradually.

Method — Rule out the wrong options

1) Read all the options carefully, and see if there are any that you can <u>rule out</u>.

   | **A** The narrator was trying to move quietly. ✗ | ← | The phrase is about the day, not the narrator, so we can discount this one. |

2) The other options seem plausible, so have a good look at how the phrase fits into the passage.

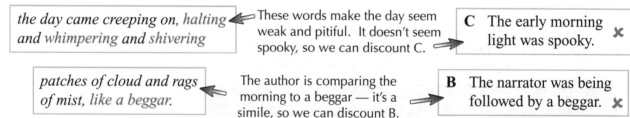

   the day came creeping on, halting and whimpering and shivering ← These words make the day seem weak and pitiful. It doesn't seem spooky, so we can discount C. → **C** The early morning light was spooky. ✗

   patches of cloud and rags of mist, like a beggar. ← The author is comparing the morning to a beggar — it's a simile, so we can discount B. → **B** The narrator was being followed by a beggar. ✗

3) This leaves us with D. → **D** It got light very gradually. ✓ ← We know that it's early morning, so the day 'creeping on' means a slow dawn.

Practice Questions

1) Write out the literal meaning of each of the following:

   a) *You're going to end up in hot water if you carry on like this.*
   b) *I put blood, sweat and tears into my maths homework.*
   c) *It's time to throw in the towel.*
   d) *I wish the politician would stop beating about the bush.*
   e) *My little brother is really driving me up the wall.*

2) *Before my eyes, the sky caught fire as the burning orb plunged into the ocean.*

   What is meant by the phrase 'the sky caught fire'?
   A It was very hot.   **B** It was sunset.
   C There was an explosion.   **D** The sky was too bright to look at.

Multiple-Statement Questions — Logic

Sometimes you need to use a bit of logic and deduction to find the answers.

Logic Questions *use lots of different skills*

To do well in logic questions you need to be able to:

1) Read and understand information and pay attention to details.

2) Pick out key pieces of information to solve a problem, and ignore the bits that are irrelevant.

3) Do simple maths quickly.

You can **Practise Logical Thinking** *in different ways*

1) Buy a puzzle magazine — these often have logic puzzles in them.
There are puzzles like this on the internet too.

2) Play games like 'Cluedo' or 'Guess Who?' to test your powers of deduction and logic.

3) Play 'Twenty Questions' with a friend — it'll help you practise dealing with information.

4) Practise doing calculations which use addition and subtraction.

11+ Style *Question*

You might be asked questions like this one in the test:

> **Q** Read the passage, then answer the question that follows.
>
> *Aileen, Pascal, Jen, Marie and Louis are talking about their cousins.*
> *Marie has 3 cousins. Jen has more cousins than Louis. Aileen has one*
> *fewer cousin than Marie. Louis has twice the number of cousins Aileen has.*
> *Pascal has no aunts or uncles.*
>
> Which one of the sentences below **cannot** be true?
>
> **A** Jen has 5 cousins.
> **B** Pascal has the fewest cousins.
> **C** Louis has 6 cousins.
> **D** Aileen is Jen's cousin.

- Only one option is definitely not true.
  You need to use the information to work out which one.

- The answer is C:

  1) You're told that Marie has three cousins.

  2) Ailleen has one fewer than Marie — so she must have two cousins.

  3) Louis has twice the number of cousins Aileen has. Aileen
     has two cousins, so Louis must have four cousins, not six.

Section Four — Comprehension

Rule out the **Options** that are definitely **Wrong**

> **Q** Read the passage, then answer the question that follows.
>
> *"Right!" exclaimed Donald. "What are the scores, Ravi Dawes?"*
> *Ravi rolled his eyes and looked down at his bit of paper listing the scores.*
> *"Looks like I've won. Donald, you got 96, but Sascha beat you by 8 points. Ola,*
> *you scored 30 less than Sascha, and Sarah, you got 78." He screwed up the bit of*
> *paper and threw it over his shoulder. "Better luck next time, boys and girls."*
>
> Which one of the sentences below **must** be true?
>
> **A** Ravi scored 110.
> **B** Ola came last.
> **C** Sascha scored less than Sarah.
> **D** Ola had never played before.

Method 1 — Look for definite facts first

1) Look at the four options. The <u>correct answer</u> will be <u>directly related</u> to the <u>information</u> in the question — <u>scan the options</u> to see if any are <u>unrelated</u>.

> ~~**D** Ola had never played before.~~ ⇐ The passage doesn't say who has played before, so you can ignore this one.

2) To <u>decide</u> between the other <u>options</u> you'll have to do some <u>maths</u> to work out what <u>each person scored</u>. First write down any <u>exact scores</u> that are given in the text.

> Donald scored 96.   Sarah scored 78.

3) Look at the <u>rest of the passage</u> and use the <u>information</u> to work out <u>each person's score</u>.

> Sascha scored 8 more than Donald. ⇒ Donald scored 96, so Sascha scored 96 + 8 = 104.
>
> Ola scored 30 less than Sascha. ⇒ Sascha scored 104, so Ola scored 104 – 30 = 74.
>
> Ravi won. ⇒ This means Ravi scored more than everyone else, so he must have scored more than 104.

4) Now you know <u>everyone's scores</u>, write them as a <u>list</u> and then <u>use the information</u> to <u>decide</u> which <u>statement is true</u>.

Ignore any options that <u>could</u> be true — you're looking for the one that <u>must</u> be true.

Write as much of each person's name as you need to — it'll stop you getting mixed up.

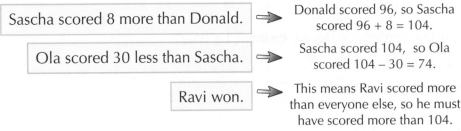

> R — 104+
> Sas — 104
> D — 96
> Sar — 78
> O — 74

> **A** Ravi scored 110. **?**
> **B** Ola came last. **✓**
> **C** Sascha scored less than Sarah. **✗**
> ~~**D** Ola had never played before.~~

5) The only statement that <u>must</u> be true is <u>B</u>.

Think about how the **Statements Fit Together**

Q Read the passage and then answer the question that follows.

Polly was meeting Stuart, Luke, Mandy and Caitlyn at the cinema.
Luke arrived before Caitlyn and Mandy. Polly arrived second.
She'd hoped to get all the girls together for a quick gossip,
but the next person to turn up was a boy.

Which one of the sentences below **cannot** be true?

   A   Stuart arrived first.
   B   Polly arrived before Luke.
   C   Mandy arrived before Polly.
   D   Caitlyn and Mandy arrived together.

Method 2 — Look at the statements one by one

1) Read the <u>passage</u>. You need to work out the <u>order</u> in which everyone <u>arrived</u>.

2) You know <u>Polly arrived second</u>. Use the <u>other statements</u> to work out <u>when</u> the <u>others arrived</u>.

   | the next person to turn up was a boy. | ⇒ Only Luke or Stuart can arrive third. |

   | Luke arrived before Caitlyn and Mandy. | ⇒ Luke must arrive first or third, so Caitlyn and Mandy must arrive fourth and fifth. If the two girls arrive fourth and fifth, Stuart can only arrive first or third. |

3) Scribble down the <u>order</u> they could <u>arrive</u>.

4) <u>Use your list</u> to <u>choose</u> the correct <u>answer</u>.
   Here you're looking for the only one that <u>cannot</u> be <u>true</u>.

5) You know <u>Mandy</u> must <u>arrive after Polly</u>, so the answer is <u>C</u>.

> 1st — L / S
> 2nd — P
> 3rd — L / S
> 4th — C / M
> 5th — C / M

Practice Question

Read the passage and then answer the question that follows.

Ellie, Mike, Nathan, Zach and Li are competing in a sack race on sports day.
Mike comes fourth. Zach isn't last. Ellie doesn't win. Li beats Zach. Nathan beats Li.

Which one of the sentences below **cannot** be true?

   A   Ellie comes last.
   B   Zach beats Mike.
   C   Ellie falls over.
   D   Li comes third.

Reasoning Questions

Reasoning questions ask you to look beyond the facts you're given in the text.

You might be asked about the **Writer's Purpose**

Q Read the passage and then answer the questions that follow.

Brushes with Nature by Hilary Powell, Tibworth Tourist Board

Award-winning wildlife painter Jack Jones opens an inspirational new exhibition in Tibworth today, charting a year in the life of a family of foxes who live at the bottom of his garden. Jack's last exhibition, 'Frogspawn', was described as 'a stunning portrayal of the transient nature of life'.

1) Why do you think the writer chose the title 'Brushes with Nature'?

A Jack Jones wants to clean up nature reserves. **B** The article is about painting.
C It sums up both of the article's topics. **D** Foxes' tails are called brushes.

Method 1 — Rule out the wrong options

1) Read through all the options carefully and <u>rule out</u> any <u>wrong</u> ones.

A Jack Jones wants to clean up nature reserves. ✗ ← The article doesn't say anything about nature reserves, so you can rule out A.

Both painting and foxes are mentioned in the article, but they're not the only reason the author chose the title, so B and D aren't right. → **B** The article is about painting. ✗
D Foxes' tails are called brushes. ✗

2) That just leaves <u>C</u>.

C It sums up both of the article's topics. ✓ ← The article is about wildlife painting, so art and nature are its topics. The title sums these up, so this is the answer.

Q 2) Why do you think the writer uses the words 'inspirational' and 'Award-winning'?

A She is a big fan of Jack Jones. **B** She wants people to visit the exhibition.
C Jack Jones inspired her to paint. **D** She really enjoyed the exhibition.

Method 2 — Look at all the evidence

1) At first glance, all these options <u>could be true</u>, but the article doesn't say that any of them <u>are</u>.

2) Sometimes, there's a bit of information <u>hidden away</u> that gives you a <u>clue</u> to the answer.

by Hilary Powell, Tibworth Tourist Board ← This gives you a big clue about why Hilary wrote the article. She works for the tourist board, so her job is to encourage people to visit Tibworth.

The exhibition could bring more people to Tibworth, so the answer is <u>B</u>. → **B** She wants people to visit the exhibition. ✓

You might have to **Work Out** how a **Character Feels**

Q Read the passage and then answer the questions that follow.

Kazim crouched behind the sofa as the footsteps approached, hardly daring to breathe. He closed his eyes and pictured the room, trying to remember whether he had left any trace of his presence. The footsteps stopped right in front of his hiding place, and Kazim jumped as a voice began to speak.

Which of these words best describes how Kazim feels?

A Disappointed   **B** Unhappy   **C** Tense   **D** Sneaky

Method — Put yourself in the character's place

1) Read the passage carefully. As you read, <u>imagine</u> you are doing what the character does. Think about <u>why</u> he's doing it, and how he might <u>feel</u>.

Kazim is hiding — he doesn't want to be seen. → Kazim crouched behind the sofa as the footsteps approached, hardly daring to breathe. ← The words 'hardly daring' show that it's a serious situation. Kazim really doesn't want to be found.

These actions don't really describe someone who is disappointed, so you can rule out A.

You'd only jump at the sound of a voice if you were on edge. → Kazim jumped as a voice began to speak

2) Look through all the <u>options</u> and pick the one that seems <u>most accurate</u>. Kazim is <u>hiding</u>, and he's <u>on edge</u>. The best adjective is '<u>tense</u>', so the answer is <u>C</u>.

Practice Questions

Read the passage and then answer the questions that follow.

The wind roared furiously around the cliffs, whipping the white-capped waves to a hissing, boiling frenzy. Leaning forward into the gale, Isla scanned the horizon feverishly. Where were they? They should have reached the far side of the lake by now. In the distance, a tiny speck of light appeared, flashed twice, and then disappeared. Isla let out a breath she didn't know she'd been holding.

1) Which of these words best describes the mood the writer creates in the passage?

   A Frightening   **B** Anxious   **C** Miserable   **D** Bitter

2) Why does Isla 'let out a breath'?

   A The wind drops, so she can breathe.   **B** She knows her friends are in danger.

   C She knows her friends are safe.   **D** She realises she is holding her breath.

Answering Comprehension Questions

There are two different types of question — multiple choice or standard answer.

Multiple Choice Questions give you Several Possible Options

1) In <u>multiple choice questions</u> you'll <u>get</u> options to choose from. You need to <u>pick</u> the <u>right answer</u>.
2) When the <u>possible options</u> are <u>similar</u>, it can make the question more <u>difficult</u>.   The best way to tackle each question is to work through it carefully, <u>step by step</u>.

Q Read the passage below. Then answer the question that follows.

1   The problem was not that the film was three hours long, or that the acting was

2   atrocious, but that the plot was incomprehensible. I have no idea what Captain Jutter

3   had to do with anything, partly because I could not understand a word he said, but also

4   because he disappeared halfway through the film, without any explanation. I don't

5   think it was ever explained exactly why the pirates had to get back to Shadow Island;

6   all I know is that it was of "great importance". The screenwriter, Jordan Vidal, needs

7   to take a long, hard look in the mirror after this terrible mishap of an adventure film.

1) According to the passage, what was the film's biggest flaw?

   A The screenwriter was not very good.
   B The acting was terrible.
   C It didn't make any sense.
   D It was too long.

> *Be wary of options that are mentioned in the text but don't answer the question, as they could mislead you. Always double-check that your answer matches the text.*

Method 1 — Find the important information

1) First, look for any <u>key words</u> relating to the question (you may have highlighted them during your first read-through):

'problem' means a similar thing to 'flaw'. → *The problem was not that the film was three hours long, or that the acting was atrocious, but that the plot was incomprehensible.* ← This sentence mentions three possible answers to the question.

The sentence tells you that the problem was not the length of the film or the acting, so it cannot be option B or D.

2) <u>Check</u> this information <u>against the options</u>.

   A The screenwriter was not very good.
   B ~~The acting was terrible~~.
   C It didn't make any sense.
   D ~~It was too long~~.

Option C is closest in meaning to the text — 'incomprehensible' means 'doesn't make any sense'.

3) <u>Double-check</u> you haven't <u>missed anything</u> else. The last line of the passage does suggest that the screenwriter was not very good (option A), but C is still the <u>best answer</u>.

Use Your Own Words for *Standard Answer Questions*

1) <u>Standard answer comprehension questions</u> aren't <u>too different</u> from multiple choice questions.

2) You can find the answers in the <u>same way</u>, but instead of choosing a given answer, you need to put it into your <u>own words</u> and write in <u>full sentences</u>.

You'll probably get multiple choice options in the test, but it's worth knowing how to answer standard answer questions too.

3) <u>Read</u> the <u>extract</u> on p.58, and then look at the question below.

 Q 2) Explain why the writer found the plot "incomprehensible" (line 2).

Method 2 — Ask yourself questions as you're reading

1) First, work out <u>what information</u> the question is asking you for:

Explain why the writer found the plot "incomprehensible" (line 2)?

This gives you a clue to where to start looking for the answer.

This tells you that you're looking for reasons why the writer didn't understand the story.

2) You should <u>start</u> by looking at the part of the text <u>mentioned</u> in the <u>question</u>:

I have no idea what Captain Jutter had to do with anything, partly because I could not understand a word he said, but also because he disappeared halfway through the film, without any explanation.

This sentence comes straight after the writer mentions that the story was "incomprehensible".

Finding key words will help you work out what's important.

This sentence tells you that the writer <u>did not know why</u> Captain Jutter was in the film, because he <u>could not understand</u> what he said, and he <u>disappeared</u> halfway through.

3) After looking around line 2, you should then <u>check</u> the <u>key words</u> in the <u>rest of the text</u>:

I don't think it was ever explained exactly why the pirates had to get back to Shadow Island...

The word 'explained' suggests that this sentence relates to the plot.

4) After you have <u>all the information</u>, you need to <u>rewrite</u> it in <u>full sentences</u>, in your <u>own words</u>:

The plot was "incomprehensible" because the writer did not know why Captain Jutter was in the film, and found it impossible to understand him. The writer was also confused because Captain Jutter vanished in the middle of the film, and it was not explained why the pirates needed to go to Shadow Island.

Quoting from the question helps focus your answer.

Change the wording so you're not just copying the text.

5) Use the <u>number of marks</u> and <u>space available</u> for your answer as a guide for <u>how much</u> to write.

Tips and Tricks for Comprehension Questions

Try to answer every question. If you're not really sure what the answer is, make a sensible guess at it because you might still get it right. Don't spend too long on one question though — you need to use your time wisely.

Comprehension Question Practice

Now that you know about answering comprehension questions, it's time for some practice.
There are some multiple choice questions on the next page.

Q Read the passage and then answer the following questions.

1   *The small boys rushed in again. Closing, they saw, was their best chance, and Flashman*
was wilder and more flurried than ever: he caught East by the throat, and tried to force him back
on the iron-bound table. Tom grasped his waist, and remembering the old throw he
had learned in the Vale from Harry Winburn, crooked his leg inside Flashman's, and threw
5   *his whole weight forward. The three tottered for a moment, and then over they went on to*
the floor, Flashman striking his head against a form in the hall.
The two youngsters sprang to their legs, but he lay there still. They began to be frightened.
Tom stooped down, and then cried out, scared out of his wits, "He's bleeding awfully.
Come here, East, Diggs — he's dying!"
10   *"Not he," said Diggs, getting leisurely off the table; "it's all sham; he's only afraid to fight it out."*
East was as frightened as Tom. Diggs lifted Flashman's head, and he groaned.
"What's the matter?" shouted Diggs.
"My skull's fractured," sobbed Flashman.
"Oh, let me run for the housekeeper!" cried Tom. "What shall we do?"
15   *"Fiddlesticks! It's nothing but the skin broken," said the relentless Diggs, feeling his head.*
"Cold water and a bit of rag's all he'll want."
"Let me go," said Flashman surlily, sitting up; "I don't want your help."
"We're really very sorry —" began East.
"Hang your sorrow!" answered Flashman, holding his handkerchief to the place;
20   *"You shall pay for this, I can tell you, both of you." And he walked out of the hall.*
"He can't be very bad," said Tom with a deep sigh, much relieved to see his enemy march so well.
"Not he," said Diggs; "and you'll see you won't be troubled with him any more.
But, I say, your head's broken too; your collar is covered with blood."
"Is it though?" said Tom, putting up his hand; "I didn't know it."
25   *"Well, mop it up, or you'll have your jacket spoilt. And you have got a nasty eye, Scud.*
You'd better go and bathe it well in cold water."
"Cheap enough too, if we've done with our old friend Flashey," said East, as they made off
upstairs to bathe their wounds.
They had done with Flashman in one sense, for he never laid finger on either of them again.

From 'Tom Brown's Schooldays' by Thomas Hughes

Practice Questions

1) Which word best describes Flashman's mood at the start of the passage?

   A Panicked   **B** Upset   **C** Frenzied   **D** Confused

2) According to the passage, which statement is true?

   A Diggs is involved in the fight.
   B Scud is the same person as East.
   C Harry is a good fighter.
   D Flashman fractures his skull.

3) What does the word "surlily" (line 17) mean?

   A Dizzily   **B** Violently   **C** Sadly   **D** Grumpily

4) What does Tom mean when he says, "He can't be very bad" (line 21)?

   A Flashman is a nice person.
   B Flashman only has a minor injury.
   C Flashman is not very good at fighting.
   D Flashman is worried about getting into trouble.

5) Who is Tom's "enemy" (line 21)?

   A The housekeeper   **B** Diggs   **C** Harry Winburn   **D** Flashman

6) How do you think Tom feels when he realises he is injured?

   A Angry, because Flashman has hurt him.
   B Scared, because he has lost a lot of blood.
   C Calm, because it was worth it to beat Flashman.
   D Pleased, because he will have a scar to show off.

7) What does Flashman mean when he says "Hang your sorrow!" (line 19)?

   A He accepts East's apology.
   B He doesn't want an apology.
   C He thinks East should apologise more convincingly.
   D He wants the other boys to apologise too.

Glossary

adjective	A word that describes a noun, e.g. 'beautiful morning', 'frosty lawn'.
adverb	A word that describes a verb, and often ends with the suffix '-ly', e.g. 'She laughed happily.', 'He ran quickly.'
antonym	A word that has the opposite meaning to another word, e.g. the antonym of 'good' is 'bad'.
connective	A word or phrase that joins two clauses or sentences, e.g. 'and', 'but', 'as soon as'.
consonants	The 21 letters of the alphabet that aren't vowels.
fiction	Text that has been made up by the author, about imaginary people and events.
homographs	Words that are spelt the same but have different meanings, e.g. 'I want to play.' and 'I saw a play.'
homophones	Words that sound the same, but mean different things, e.g. 'hair' and 'hare'.
imagery	Language that creates a vivid picture in the reader's mind.
metaphor	A way of describing something by saying that it is something else, e.g. 'John's legs were lead weights.'
multiple choice	A type of 11+ question that gives you answers to choose from.
non-fiction	Text that is about facts and real people and events.
noun	A word that names something, e.g. 'Paul', 'cat', 'fear', 'childhood'.
personification	A way of describing something by giving it human feelings and characteristics, e.g. 'The cruel wind plucked remorselessly at my threadbare clothes.'
prefix	A string of letters that can be put in front of a word to change its meaning, e.g. 'un-' can be added to 'lock' to make 'unlock'.
pronoun	A word that can be used instead of a noun, e.g. 'I', 'you', 'he', 'it'.
simile	A way of describing something by comparing it to something else, e.g. 'The stars were like a thousand diamonds, glittering in the sky.'
subject	The person or thing doing the action of a verb, e.g. 'Jo laughed.', 'The bird flew.'
suffix	A string of letters that can be put after a word to change its meaning, e.g. '-er' can be added to the end of 'play' to make 'player'.
synonym	A word with a similar meaning to another word, e.g. 'big' is a synonym of 'huge'.
verb	An action or doing word, e.g. 'run', 'went', 'think', or a being word, e.g. 'is'.
vowels	The letters 'a', 'e', 'i', 'o' and 'u'.

Answers

PAGES 4-5 — PREPARING FOR THE TEST

1) **a)** Various answers possible, e.g. 'de-', 'ex-', 'mis-', 'post-' and 'pre-'.

These aren't the only possible answers. If you've got a different answer, you can check it in a dictionary.

2) **a)** Various answers possible, e.g. 'stroke', 'string', 'strict', 'stripe'.

   b) No. There are no words in English which begin with 'blr'.

   c) Various answers possible, e.g. 'shrink', 'shrub', 'shrug', 'shrine'.

   d) No. There are no words in English which begin with 'ds'.

Some combinations of letters never appear in English.

3) **a)** anywhere

   b) stubborn

   c) hovercraft

   d) shipwreck

These are the correct spellings of these words.

4) **a)** unnatural

   b) angrily

   c) misspell

   d) vaccinate

If a word ends in a vowel or a 'y', you'll usually have to take the last letter off before adding the suffix. If the word ends in a vowel followed by a 'y', you don't take off the last letter.

PAGES 6-7 — PLURALS

1) **a)** The plural of 'branch' is 'branches'.

   b) The plural of 'foot' is 'feet'.

   c) The plural of 'Grady' is 'Gradys'.

   d) The plural of 'wolf' is 'wolves'.

   e) The plural of 'dress' is 'dresses'.

Words ending with 'ch' or 's' usually take an 'es' plural, and words ending with 'y' usually take an 'ies' plural unless it is a proper noun.

PAGES 8-9 — HOMOPHONES AND HOMOGRAPHS

Warm-Up Activity

'piece' sounds like 'peace'.
'waist' sounds like 'waste'.
'or' sounds like 'oar', 'ore' and 'awe'.
'sale' sounds like 'sail'.
'sight' sounds like 'site' and 'cite'.
'male' sounds like 'mail'.

Practice Questions

1) I'm supposed to go to drama group every Monday **night**, but this **week** I'm too tired. I've had a very busy day at school and I'm not feeling **great**. Instead, I think I'm going to stay **here** and watch a film that I haven't **seen** before.

The words in bold are the correct homophones.

2) **a)** Make sure that you know **where** you are going.

   b) Watch out for the crab — it has very sharp **claws**.

   c) At the theme park, we **rode** on four different roller coasters.

   d) The jockey pulled on the **reins** to get the horse to stop.

The correct answer should have a meaning which fits the context.

PAGES 10-11 — PREFIXES AND SUFFIXES

Warm-Up Activity

'un' and 'available' make 'unavailable'.
'thought' and 'ful' make 'thoughtful'.
'formal' and 'ly' make 'formally'.
'work' and 'er' make 'worker'.

Practice Questions

1) **a)** The baby polar bear is so **adorable**.

   b) I was trying to be **helpful** when I washed the dishes.

   c) The ball hit Kayley and knocked her **unconscious**.

   d) Lyla's feeling of **happiness** increased when she found her shoes.

   e) The apple was covered in mould and the flesh was **rotten**.

The prefix and suffixes which have been added all fit the context of the sentences.

PAGES 12-13 — SILENT LETTERS AND DOUBLE LETTERS

Warm-Up Activity

In 'knife' the silent consonant is 'k'.

In 'scene' the silent consonant is 'c'.

In 'gnome' the silent consonant is 'g'.

In 'island' the silent consonant is 's'.

In 'while' the silent consonant is 'h'.

In 'lamb' the silent consonant is 'b'.

In 'rhyme' the silent consonant is 'h'.

Practice Questions

1) a) I **maintained** a comfortable position for the whole journey.

   b) You need to wear more **clothes** in winter to keep warm.

   c) My **interesting** entry will win the competition tomorrow.

Make sure that double letters have been used correctly .

2) a) Everyone agreed that the charity event had been **successful**.

   b) While we're in London, we want to visit Nelson's **Column**.

   c) Sasha is the most **intelligent** girl in the class.

   d) I arrived just as the show was **beginning**.

These are the correct spellings of each word.

PAGES 14-15 — OTHER AWKWARD SPELLINGS

1) a) My car is running out of **diesel**.

   b) Don't forget to paint the **ceiling**.

   c) Mr Harris went to the museum to see the **ancient** remains.

Use the rule "'i' before 'e' except after 'c', but only when it rhymes with bee" to help you to work out the correct spellings.

2) a) The missing letter in 'desp**e**rate' is 'e'.

   b) The missing letter in 'fact**o**ry' is 'o'.

   c) The missing letter in 'respons**i**ble' is 'i'.

   d) The missing letter in 'harm**o**ny' is 'o'.

   e) The missing letters in 'lit**era**ture' are 'e' and 'a'.

   f) The missing letter in 'pass**a**ge' is 'a'.

These are the vowels needed to correctly spell each word.

PAGES 16-17 — PREPARING FOR WORD MEANING QUESTIONS

1) a) 'sang' is a verb

   b) 'honesty' is a noun (an abstract noun)

   c) 'nosy' is an adjective

   d) 'tighten' is a verb

   e) 'cryptic' is an adjective

   f) 'play' can either be a verb or a noun

   g) 'vacantly' is an adverb

2) a) 'truth' is an abstract noun that means 'the reality of a matter'.

   b) 'cantankerous' is an adjective that means 'grumpy' or 'disagreeable'.

   c) 'wrathfully' is an adverb that means 'angrily'.

   d) 'bemusement' is a noun that means 'confusion'.

Verbs are doing words, nouns are things, adjectives describe nouns and adverbs describe verbs.

PAGES 18-19 — MULTIPLE MEANINGS

Warm-Up Activity

Various answers possible, e.g.
Rich — 'wealthy' or 'creamy or heavy'.
Ruler — 'a measuring device' or 'the leader of a group of people.'
Match — 'a piece of wood you strike to create fire' or 'a sporting competition'.
Fly — 'a winged insect' or 'to move through the air'.
Row — 'an argument' or 'to paddle a boat'.

Practice Questions

1) a) talk

'talk' can mean 'a presentation' or 'to converse'.

   b) run

'run' can mean 'to be in charge' or 'to move quickly'.

   c) book

'book' can mean 'to arrange something' or 'something you read'.

PAGES 20-23 — CLOSEST MEANING

Warm-Up Activity

The words fit together in the following way:

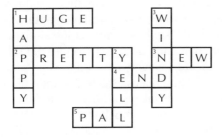

Practice Questions

1) a) petrified

Both of these mean 'very scared'.

b) track

Both of these mean 'a path' or 'to follow something'

c) beamed

Both of these mean 'grinned'.

2) a) l**a**mp

b) n**o**vel

c) l**e**ap

Look at the letters you're given and think about whether the missing letters are more likely to be vowels or consonants. In the example of 'lamp', you know 'l' is rarely followed by a consonant at the start of a word, so the second letter must be a vowel.

PAGES 24-27 — OPPOSITE MEANING

Warm-Up Activity

Various answers possible, but can include any words with opposite meanings, e.g. happy — sad; poor — rich; serious — jokey; dainty — hefty.

Practice Questions

1) a) absent

'present' means 'here', whereas 'absent' means 'away'

b) defend

'accuse' means 'to blame someone', whereas 'defend' means 'to argue someone's case'.

c) abolish

'establish' means 'to start something' whereas 'abolish' means 'to end something'.

2) a) l**a**te

b) rig**h**t

c) so**f**t

The letters in bold are the missing letters.

PAGES 28-29 — ODD ONE OUT

Warm-Up Activity

Various answers possible, but can include:
Capital cities — London, Paris, Tokyo
Vegetables — carrots, leeks, courgettes
Animals that live in the sea — lobsters, jellyfish, octopuses

Practice Questions

1) peaceful

The other three all mean 'boring'.

2) novel

The other three are non-fiction texts.

3) dormant

The other three all mean 'feeling tired'.

4) morose

The other three all mean 'happy'.

PAGES 30-31 — REORDER WORDS TO MAKE A SENTENCE

Warm-Up Activity

Various answers possible, e.g.
The farmer milked his <u>cows</u> in the <u>barn</u>.
I <u>ate</u> my pizza while I <u>read</u> my book.
Josephine has <u>red</u> hair and <u>blue</u> eyes.

Practice Questions

1) are

The sentence is — 'Jo is the happiest girl I know'.

2) rock

The sentence is — 'The walrus dived into the sea and caught a fish'.

3) field

The sentence is — 'Take the footpath if you want to get there quickly'.

PAGES 32-33 — PREPARING FOR CLOZE QUESTIONS

Practice Questions

1) a) It was getting **dark**, so I turned on the light.

b) Harry fell off the camel and **landed** on his feet.

c) Playing basketball **improves** your coordination.

The words in bold are the correct answers.

2) **a)** Chen and Beth ran away from the **ug**ly monster.

b) I go swimming with my frie**nd**s every Monday night.

c) My dog won't stop scratching — I think he has **flea**s.

The letters in bold are the missing letters.

PAGES 34-35 — USING RULES OF ENGLISH — VERBS

Practice Questions

1) **a)** Barney has **eaten** all of my popcorn.

b) I have **been** to South Africa on holiday.

c) Barry's knee is **hurting** after he fell over.

d) You should **go** home or you'll be late.

e) What time do you think you will **arrive**?

f) The dolphin is about to **leap** out of the water.

The words in bold are the correct answers. Read the sentence out loud to help you find the right answer.

PAGES 36-37 — USING RULES OF ENGLISH — CONNECTIVES

Practice Questions

The Amazon Rainforest covers 40% of South America, <u>although</u> it has decreased in size. Humans have cut down the trees <u>because</u> they need wood for construction <u>and</u> space to build farms. <u>However</u>, conservation efforts are under way to protect the rainforest <u>and</u> stop people from illegally cutting down the trees.

The words that are underlined are the connectives.

2) **a)** I really like to eat cereal for breakfast. **However**, I sometimes eat a slice of toast.

b) I'd like to go out to the Italian restaurant tonight, **although** Chinese is my favourite.

c) We went to play hockey, **despite** the rain.

The words in bold are the correct answers. Look at the context to find the right connective.

PAGES 38-41 — ANSWERING CLOZE QUESTIONS

Practice Questions

1) At **up** to thirty metres long, blue whales are **approximately** three times the **length** of a double-decker bus. These **colossal** marine mammals eat four to eight tonnes of krill, tiny sea creatures, **every** day. Blue whales have a fringe of fine plates **attached** to their upper jaw. To feed, they **take** in a huge mouthful of water and force it out **through** the fringe. The krill are too **big** to pass between the plates, **so** they stay in the whale's mouth.

The words in bold are the correct answers.

2) With a groan, the sol**die**r came to. His head felt as th**ough** someone had been using it as a football. With a grunt of p**ai**n, he scrambled to his feet and wa**ite**d for the sky to stop its alarming spinning. He bent slowly and picked up his rifle, then stumbled o**nw**ard. His inj**ure**d ankle made it difficult to walk quickly, but he knew he had to reach the tr**en**ch before the next round of shelling st**arte**d. He was so close — he could almost reach out and touch the bank of ea**rth** that marked the edge of the ditch. Just a few more paces and he would reach safety and **shelt**er.

The letters in bold are the missing letters.

PAGES 42-43 — READING THE TEXT

Practice Questions

1) **a)** Eric Debuski's stage name is Lavahead.

b) The word "frontman" (line 6) can mean the same thing as "lead vocalist".

c) Joaquin works in a shop — in the passage it says that "he scanned through Eric's basket", which means that he was working on a till.

d) Eric tells Joaquin to shut his mouth because he was probably gaping at meeting a member of his favourite band.

e) Joaquin stutters and Eric tells him to shut his mouth, probably because he is gaping. This shows he is feeling nervous. He also says it was "the most exciting thing that had happened", which shows how thrilled he was.

Try to mention all of the relevant information when you're writing an answer to a comprehension question.

PAGES 46-47 — FINDING HIDDEN FACTS

Practice Questions

1) Marta

Marta sees a pedestrian, a cat, a tractor and a cyclist.

2) Four

Glen is the only child who does not see a motorised vehicle. Kim sees a car, Marta sees a tractor and Ali sees both.

PAGES 48-49 — WORD MEANINGS

Practice Questions

1) A

'Fervently' means 'with great passion or emotion'.

2) D

'Circumspect' means 'aware of possible consequences', which is closest in meaning to 'cautious'.

PAGES 50-52 — UNDERSTANDING THE LANGUAGE IN THE TEXT

Practice Questions

1) **a)** You're going to end up in trouble if you carry on like this.

b) I put a lot of effort into my maths homework.

c) It's time to give up.

d) I wish the politician would stop avoiding the issue.

e) My little brother is really annoying me.

Answers may vary for these questions, but make sure you have given the literal meaning for each sentence.

2) B

The phrase "the sky caught fire" describes the colour of the sky. You can tell that it is sunset because the passage says 'the burning orb [the Sun] plunged into the ocean'.

PAGES 53-55 — MULTIPLE-STATEMENT QUESTIONS — LOGIC

Practice Questions

1) D

Nathan beat Li, and Li beat Zach. Zach didn't come last, and he can't have come fourth because Mike came fourth. This means that Zach must have come third and Li must have come second.

PAGES 56-57 — REASONING QUESTIONS

Practice Questions

1) B

The writer asks "Where were they?" and says that Isla "scanned the horizon feverishly". This shows how anxious Isla was, which makes the reader feel worried too.

2) C

Isla has been holding her breath because she is so worried about her friends. The flashing light is a sign that they are safe, so she relaxes.

PAGES 60-61 — COMPREHENSION QUESTION PRACTICE

Practice Questions

1) C

The passage says that Flashman was "wilder and more flurried than ever" (line 2).

2) B

Scud is the same person as East. There are only three people involved in the fight: Tom, Flashman and East. At the end of the extract Diggs says, "And you have got a nasty eye, Scud" (line 25), and East replies, which suggests that "East" and "Scud" are different names for the same person.

3) D

'Surlily' means the same as 'grumpily'.

4) B

Tom says "He can't be very bad" after seeing Flashman walk away "so well" (line 21). This suggests Tom thinks that Flashman's injury is not very bad.

5) D

Tom's "enemy" is Flashman.

6) C

Tom says that he hadn't noticed his injury, which shows that he's not angry or scared. East says that their injuries were "Cheap enough", showing that the boys' main concern is that they beat Flashman.

7) B

Flashman doesn't want an apology. He says that the other boys will "pay for this", which shows that he's interested in revenge, not making up.

Index

VHRDF1